Joseph Hatton

The New Ceylon

Being a sketch of British North Borneo, or Sabah

Joseph Hatton

The New Ceylon
Being a sketch of British North Borneo, or Sabah

ISBN/EAN: 9783337244125

Printed in Europe, USA, Canada, Australia, Japan

Cover: Foto ©ninafisch / pixelio.de

More available books at **www.hansebooks.com**

KINA BALU, BRITISH NORTH BORNEO.

(From a Sketch by Lord Elphinstone.)

"THE NEW CEYLON."

BEING A SKETCH OF

BRITISH NORTH BORNEO, OR SABAH.

FROM OFFICIAL
AND OTHER EXCLUSIVE SOURCES OF INFORMATION.

WRITTEN AND COMPILED BY

JOSEPH HATTON

(AUTHOR OF "TO-DAY IN AMERICA," ETC. ETC.).

With New and Original Maps corrected to date.

LONDON:

CHAPMAN AND HALL, LIMITED,

11, HENRIETTA STREET, COVENT GARDEN.

1881.

CHARLES DICKENS AND EVANS,
CRYSTAL PALACE PRESS.

PREFACE.

"Any more for the Continental express?"

The electric lamps "flashed into a sudden radiance" as the sun is said to do at daybreak in the tropics.

For a few minutes previously to the simultaneous leap of light that transformed a dozen opaque globes into mimic suns, Charing Cross railway station had been in semi-darkness.

There was much bustle of departing travellers. Parliament was up; for even the longest and most obstructed session comes to an end. Jaded legislators, men of fashion, ladies of society, were among the crowd bound for foreign shores. London was emptying itself from all its avenues of transit.

"Any more for the Continental express?" shouted the platform inspector.

A banging of doors, a shrill whistle, a last pressure of hands through carriage-windows, and the red lamps of the Express for a moment challenged the white sentinels of Electra, only to leave the spectators gazing at the glistening track of steel along which it vanished into the outer darkness.

They were no mere holiday travellers, the two

young men whose latest adieux were made to me.
Their guns were not to be loaded for sport on Scotch
moors. They were pioneers bound for the Eastern
seas. Adventurers had gone before, and smoothed
the rugged way for the allied aid of science, which
London and Edinburgh now contributed to North
Borneo, the one a chemist, metallurgical and otherwise, the other a doctor of medicine. Ahead of them
were a respected Governor, a staff of officials and
four years of diplomatic history, with a royal charter
of her Gracious Majesty Queen Victoria to follow.

It was, as I have already intimated, the autumn
time of year, when the sadness of empty houses falls
with strange impressiveness upon the West-End
streets. The dull windows shed no illumination upon
the languid traffic of the finished season. There is
nothing more solemn than an empty house, more
especially that which has been tenanted by your own
family circle. Run up to town from your vacation
retreat and note the pathetic dumbness of your
" household gods." It is an experience in sensations.
And how terribly empty is a familiar room when the
familiar friend has left it, not to return for years !

Such a room stands wide open near to the desk
upon which I am writing. It contains a chest of
empty pigeon-holes, each docketed with scientific
titles; a nest of shelves crowded with the transactions of learned Societies and technical works
on mineralogy, metallurgy, and geology; a desk
stained with many acids; a broken blowpipe; a

pair of foils; a photograph of Professor Huxley; a kindly letter from Dr. Frankland; a cabinet of minerals in the rough; a barometer; and in one dark corner a package of miscellaneous books, papers, and manuscripts, relating to the sun-lands above which tower the sacred heights of Kina Balu. In that empty room (the relics of its former occupation of which are so eloquent to me, and may be to some of my readers) a student of the Royal School of Mines burnt the midnight oil. Recent investigations into the influence of bacteria on gases and kindred subjects gained for him considerable distinction at the Institute of Chemistry and the Chemical Society of London, and were recognised in the scientific organs of Germany and America. These labours may be said to have closed his student career. Endorsed by the best authorities, he was selected by the Governors of the new colony to explore its mineral resources.

We had studied these books and papers together, he and I, and had thus been enabled to see, through the eyes of many travellers, those almost unknown lands of tropical splendour to which the pioneers have gone. Since then a further collection of private letters and explorers' reports have been lent to me— official documents, and letters of interesting experiences. It is believed by certain friends of mine that, with this exceptional material at my disposal, I may compile and write a book of practical value (a pioneer volume, let me call it) upon the new colony and the newest British charter. The Directors have given me

access to their correspondence upon the subject. In
addition to this epistolary history, I shall avail myself
of the best-written sources of information that bear
upon the plan and object of the work in hand, the
intention of which is to set forth the position and
prospects of the new colony, and to tell the story of the
East India Company's nineteenth-century successor.

While I sit before that pile of books and papers,
from which the romantic story of the tropical island
and its northern colony is to be extracted, the
Continental express has transferred its travellers to
foreign boat and train. Before I have analysed half
of my collection of letterpress and manuscript, the
former occupant of the empty room will have stood
face to face with Nature in her most lovely and yet
most strange and startling forms. Sabah has been
described as an earthly paradise. The simile may
hold good, from a British point of view, when the
owners have built piers and roads and villages there
on approved models ; when the planter is on the spot
and the new colonist is sowing his rice; when the
cooling breezes of Kina Balu waft the punkahs of hill
residences, and the wild "gardens of the sun" are
cultivated tracts of fruits and flowers. This time will
no doubt come ; and then the pioneers may rest, and
we will talk no more of empty rooms.

JOSEPH HATTON.

14, Titchfield Terrace,
      Regent's Park, London,
            November, 1881.

CONTENTS.

I.

A NEW COLONY BY ROYAL CHARTER.

II.

LANDS OF PERPETUAL SUMMER.

VI.

RIGHT ACROSS BORNEO.

VII.

THE PIONEERS AT WORK.

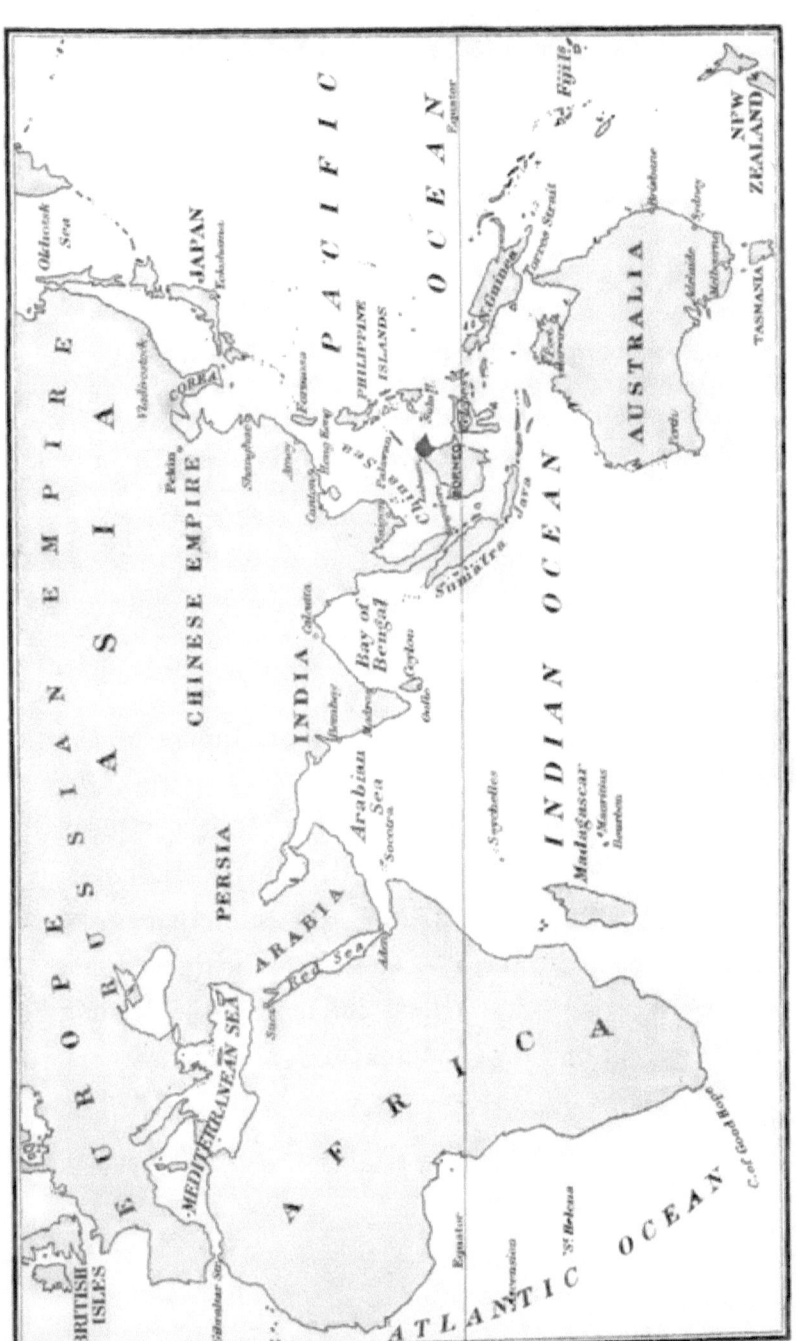

London : Published for the British North Borneo Company, by Edward Stanford, 55 Charing Cross.

THE NEW CEYLON.

I.

A NEW COLONY BY ROYAL CHARTER.

Merchant Venturers, Past and Present—Queen Elizabeth and Queen Victoria—The British North Borneo Company—Treaties with the Sultans of Brunei and Sooloo—Declaring the New Rulers—Appointment of Residents—Administering Justice—Trade Guarantees—The Smallest British Colony and the Newest Private Enterprise—Points for the Royal Charter—Unexplored Territory—A New Era in the History of Colonisation—Fresh Fields for the Tropical Planter.

I.

A NEW flag has been added to the banners of the English Guilds.

The latest charter signed by her Majesty Queen Victoria, while it links to-day with the splendid enterprises that distinguished the reign of another great English queen, Elizabeth, demonstrates a higher sense of morality than that which influenced the trading expeditions of our first "merchant venturers."

B

,7

John and Sebastian Cabot were representative of
their day. They were empowered to plant the British
flag in any city or island they could find during their
warlike progresses round about the world. On these
early lines England built up a great empire. It has been
held together in this more civilised age by a policy of
administration, the characteristic of which has been
a liberal recognition of the rights of the conquered
and a proper regard for the duties and responsibilities
of the conqueror. It may indeed be fairly said that,
during the present reign, by the civilising mission of
education, roads, bridges, railways, encouragement of
native trades and justice to native aspirations, England
has redeemed the harshness that attached to some of
her first transactions with the people whose territories
she violently annexed, and whose liberties she violently
controlled.

The old days of warlike conquest are over for
this country. England does not seek to extend
her empire by fire and sword. Now and then,
struggling peoples, petitioning to come within the
pale of British protection, are permitted the privileges of our commonwealth of colonies and possessions; but the approved policy of the age seems to be
the maintenance of that which already belongs to us,
and the promotion of its complete development. At
the same time, looking for new markets for our

trade, we are ready by international treaties and engagements to facilitate the freedom of our business operations, to increase the number of our mercantile ports and stations, and extend the empire of our commerce. As a nation we must always be peculiarly sensitive in regard to mercantile or political movements affecting the progress of the East. The absorption of North Borneo, its government, its natural resources, its soil, and its splendid possibilities, by a British company is therefore of peculiar interest and importance.*

* "In looking over the map of the world it is a melancholy reflection to view so large a portion of the habitable globe as all Borneo abandoned to barbarism and desolation; that, with all her productive wealth and advantages of physical situation, her valuable and interesting shores should have been overlooked by all Europeans; that neither the Dutch nor the Portuguese, with centuries of uncontrolled power in these seas, should have shed a ray of civilisation on shores bordering upon their principal settlements; that her ports and rivers, instead of affording a shelter to the extensive commerce of China, should at this enlightened period of the world hold out only terror and dismay to the mariner; and that all that she should have acquired from the deadly vicinage and withering grasp of Dutch power and dominion has been the art of more speedily destroying each other, and rendering themselves obnoxious to the rest of mankind. Now that her destinies are transferred to the enlightened heads and liberal hearts of Englishmen, now that her fortunes are embarked under the administration of a wise and liberal government, we may confidently hope that a happier order of things will, under the blessing of an all-ruling Providence, speedily restore these extensive shores to peace, to plenty, and to commerce; and we ardently trust that another age may not be suffered to pass away

Merchants and traders of the City of London, before
and since the halcyon days of Sir Thomas Gresham,
have been celebrated for their far-reaching enterprise and ambition. Their determination to trade
with the East was the moving spirit of many of the
early undertakings of our great explorers. Curiously
enough, it was an incorporated society of merchant
adventurers that opened up Russia as an English
market. This commercial alliance was an incident of
the eventful reign of Elizabeth. In those days we
coupled India and China together under the name of
"Cathay," and the triumphs of Drake, Hawkins, and
Frobisher over the captains of Spain giving us, after
the destruction of the Armada, freedom of the seas
and the right to establish English colonies on American
soil, only intensified the desire of London, Bristol, and
other English ports to trade with "far Cathay."
Failing to reach India by the Polar Seas, and after
a disastrous attempt to get there through Russia,
Ralph Fitch, in 1583, reverted to the more familiar
path of previous mariners by the Mediterranean and
the Persian Gulf. He was seized and imprisoned by
the Portuguese. James Lancaster followed in 1591,
in the track of the Portuguese themselves, sailing

without exhibiting something consolatory to the statesman, the
philosopher, and philanthropist."—*Report of J. Hunt, Esq., to Sir
Stamford Raffles* (1812), *on behalf of the East India Company.*

round the Cape of Good Hope. The captain adventurer
and seven of his companions survived the disastrous
failure. Sacrifices of men and money had marked the
long history of our efforts to trade with the East, but
only to stimulate the country to fresh exertions. "The
last day of the first year of the seventeenth century,"
says Dr. Yeats, in his excellent treatise on "The Growth
and Vicissitudes of Commerce," "was signalised by the
incorporation of the Governor and Company of the
Merchants of London trading to the East Indies.
Five ships laden with merchandise were despatched
under Captain Lancaster. Their commander visited
Sumatra and Java, established factories, and returned
with freights of great value. The success of the
enterprise, which Elizabeth did not live to see, gave
promise of a vigorous growth of the new company,
without, however, foreshadowing the imperial splendour that awaited it."

Taking into consideration the height of the power
which has grown up on these foundations, and the
general competition of great nations for the command
of the world, it would, at first blush, seem as if but
little opening were left for private enterprise. But,
as Elizabeth endorsed with her bold signature the
East India Company, so has Victoria placed her royal
seal upon the British North Borneo Company, which
has established its authority in a portion of what

Hellwald and Wallace declare to be the richest group of islands in the world.

II.

Four or five years ago, Mr. Alfred Dent, a member of the commercial house of Dent Brothers and Co., London, having a wide knowledge of the countries of the East, turned his attention to those tropical gardens of the equator, which, round about the famous Bornean range of mountains, were literally running to inglorious seed. He visited the reigning authorities, and concluded negotiations with them for the transfer of their territorial rights. The reputation of the white man stands very high with the natives of Borneo. Mr. Dent found his path smoothed still farther by the success of British rule in another part of the island under Rajah Brooke. He was therefore enabled in 1878 to make a statement and application to her Majesty's Secretary of State for Foreign Affairs, which contains a brief history of his relations with the new colony, and in which may be found the *raison d'être* of the charter.* During the whole of his intercourse

* " I confess, in taking a larger range than a merely commercial view admits, that it seems to be a matter of very great national importance that this northern part of Borneo should not pass into the hands of any other country, considering the naval supremacy we have in those seas, and that it is on the fair way to so many of our

with the Sultans, and, indeed, from the first inception of this great enterprise, Mr. Dent, and afterwards the Company, have had the benefit of the personal advice and assistance of Mr. W. H. Read, a gentleman who has resided in Singapore upwards of forty years. His name is frequently mentioned in the published letters of the late Sir James Brooke, whose friend he was, and whose system of administering through the local chiefs of Sarawak he approved. Mr. Read over a long course of years had studied the question of governing native races, and his policy has been so successful that he has earned for himself the appellation of "the friend of the native." On returning

possessions. Remembering, too, that for some 1400 miles from Singapore to Hong Kong we have not a single port where any fleet of merchant ships could find refuge in case of warfare; and that there might be the greatest possible injury, if not destruction, to our commerce and to our mercantile navy from any enemy possessing such a port as there is in Gaya, on the north-west of Borneo, within the territory now conceded. It is a magnificent port, and in these seas there is nothing until you come to Labuan, which, it is very well known, possesses only a coaling station, and affords anchorage for but a few ships. Certain it is, that if we were at war to-morrow, and an enemy had possession of the country and port now under consideration, the first thing we should have to do would be to drive them out of it. It is wiser, in my opinion, to take it when it is offered, and, extending the protection of our flag over it, to occupy the ground, than to let others take and fortify it. So that, whether you look at it commercially or politically, I consider this acquisition one of the greatest importance."—*Sir Rutherford Alcock, at the Meeting on North Borneo, March,* 1879.

recently to Singapore, after a visit to England, he was
welcomed home to the colony with marked demonstrations of esteem by all classes of the native population. After laying the foundation of the enterprise,
Mr. Dent, in the year mentioned, formed a private
association for the purpose of formally acquiring the
territorial grants for which he had engaged himself
with the reigning Sultans, and for developing the
resources of the country. The Sultan of Borneo
made three territorial grants to Mr. Dent and Baron
Overbeck (who transferred them to the Company)
all dated December 29th, 1877.

The sum and substance of the statement to the
English Government is as follows:

(a) By one he grants to the undersigned conjointly, their heirs,
associates, successors, or assigns, certain districts described, on the
north-west coast, with the islands off the coast. The districts
granted are vested in the grantees, for so long as they choose
to hold them. But a proviso is annexed, that the Sultan
has the right to resume the control and government thereof
if the annual sum agreed for is not paid for three successive
years.

(b) The second grant, which is in the like form or to the
like effect, relates to districts described, on the north-east
coast.

(c) The third grant, which is also in the like form or to the
like effect, relates to other districts on the north-west coast, with
other islands off the coast. It also comprises the province of
Pappar, stated in the grant to belong to the Sultan as his private
property.

By an instrument dated the same day, the Pangeran Tumongong of Brunei, the Sultan's minister and heir-presumptive or expected successor, made a similar grant of the provinces of Kimanis and Benoni, on the north-west coast, with the islands off the coast. These territories are set forth in the grant to belong to the grantor as his private property.

These four grants of territory are accompanied by a fifth instrument emanating from the Sultan of Brunei. This instrument is a commission of explanation and delegation in relation to the powers and privileges to be exercised and enjoyed in the granted territory. It recites first the effects of the four grants of territory; and then proceeds to make known that the Sultan has nominated and appointed the Company supreme rulers of the granted territory, with certain titles of a local character; and it enumerates their powers and rights, including full legislative and executive authority, the rights of property vested in the Sultan over the soil, rights over the productions of the country, and the right of levying customs and other dues and taxes. The enumeration ends with a general reference to all other powers and rights usually exercised by and belonging to sovereign rulers; and these the Sultan declares he thereby delegates to the Company, of his own free will.

The Sultan then, by this commission, calls on all
foreign nations with whom he has friendly treaties to
acknowledge the Company's chief representative as
himself (the Sultan) in the granted territory, and to
respect his authority therein.

III.

Before the negotiations above described, arrangements had been under discussion with the representative of an American partnership or company,
which had some years before acquired, in the manner
to be now stated, an interest in the territory so
granted to the present Company. In August, 1865,
the then United States Consul at Brunei obtained
from the Sultan of Brunei and the Pangeran Tumongong three concessions of territory in North Borneo,
including portions of the territory now in question, in
consideration of certain annual payments. These
concessions were substantially similar to the grants
now in question, but in form were leases for ten years
renewable. The lessee proceeded to form a partnership, called the American Trading Company of
Borneo, consisting entirely of Americans, including
Mr. Torrey, then in business at Hong Kong, afterwards United States Vice-Consul at Bangkok, and a

few Chinese merchants at Hong Kong. To this body the lessee transferred his leases. In November, 1866, the Sultan issued another instrument, which was countersigned by all his regular ministers, reciting these leases, and the transfer of them, and the lessee's request that the authority under them might be vested in his partners in the American Trading Company; and then going on to appoint certain offices, with local titles, and to confer on him, as president of that company, large powers and rights of government and property. The American partnership or company proceeded to enter into trading operations on the coast; and, with the assistance of Chinese workmen and coolies imported from Hong Kong, they formed a settlement on the Kimanis River, on the north-west coast, about sixty miles from Labuan. But from want of capital the partnership did not flourish; the settlement broke up, the Chinese colonists returned to China; and no other attempt at the formation of establishments was made, the further operations of the partnership being limited to occasional trading ventures on the coast. They then became desirous to dispose of their leases and powers. Thereupon, Baron Overbeck, who afterwards represented Mr. Dent's association, entered into an agreement with Mr. Torrey, as president of and sole surviving

partner in the American partnership or company (for
himself, and on behalf of the partnership and their
representatives, and all persons interested therein),
for the sale and transfer of all the rights and
interests of the American partnership in the territories and leases, with the exclusive right to use
the name or title of the American partnership. In
May, 1875, he went to Brunei with Mr. Torrey. He
there communicated with the Sultan and leading
chiefs, in order to ascertain from them directly
whether they considered the American leases still
in force; and in course of various interviews, in
which the Sultan and chiefs recognised the validity
of the leases, the English representative satisfied
himself that the leases had been made after friendly
negotiations, freely, without pressure or coercion,
and for good pecuniary considerations. When in
1877 he returned to Brunei and obtained the grants
now in question for the Association, Mr. Torrey
again accompanied him, in order to convince the
Sultan and chiefs that the new arrangement was
being concluded with the approval of the holders
of the American leases.

The Sultan of Brunei and Pangeran Tumongong
have received from Mr. Dent an agreed sum in
settlement of all claims on their part under the
American leases.

IV.

In addition to the four grants from the Sultan of
Brunei, Mr. Dent and his associates have obtained
from the Sultan of Sooloo one grant of territory, dated
22nd January, 1878. Thereby, on behalf of himself, his
heirs and successors, and with the consent and advice
of the Datoos in council assembled, the Sultan grants,
of his own free and sovereign will, to the British
Company, cojointly, their heirs, associates, successors,
and assigns in perpetuity, his rights and powers over
the territories tributary to him on the mainland, with
certain limits therein specified, with the islands off
the coast. In consideration of this grant they
undertake to pay to him, his heirs or successors,
5000 dollars a-year. The granted territory is thereby vested in the grantees for as long as they desire
to hold it. The grant contains a proviso that the
rights and privileges conferred thereby shall never
be transferred to any other nation, or company of
foreign nationality, without the sanction of her
Britannic Majesty's Government first obtained. It
also declares that if a dispute arises between the
Sultan and the Company, it shall be submitted to
the British Consul-General for Borneo.

The two provisions last stated are additional to those contained in the grants from the Sultan of Brunei. They were added on the suggestion of her Majesty's then Acting Consul-General for Borneo.

The territory granted by the Sultan of Sooloo is part of that granted by the Sultan of Brunei. Such portion of the territory as purports to be granted by both was considered as under the control of the Sultan of Sooloo, but the Sultan of Brunei asserted an ancient claim to the sovereignty of it. An examination of the validity of this claim would have seriously delayed the arrangements; it was therefore thought expedient, on behalf of the Association, to have grants from both the Sultans.

The Sultan of Sooloo has also granted a commission of explanation, and of delegation of powers and rights of government and legislation, and of property, corresponding with the commission above described as issued by the Sultan of Brunei.

In order to convey to the natives information of the grants, each of the two Sultans deputed a high officer to accompany the representative of the Association in a voyage round the coast. At each of the places touched at, these native officers assembled the chiefs and people, and read to them a solemn proclamation of their Sultan, announcing the grants, and exhorting and commanding them to obey the new authorities. This was done at six different places, and everywhere the news was received in a friendly spirit.

v.

The Company, therefore, has satisfied the sovereigns of the country; no coercion or undue pressure has been used; and reasonable pecuniary arrangements have been made. They have also satisfied the local chiefs and native populations on the coast. Moreover, they had come to terms with the only possible rival claimants, namely, the American Company. They therefore proceeded to act under their grants. At three of the principal points on the coast, small permanent establishments were forthwith established, namely, Sandakan, Tampassuk, and Pappar.

These stations demonstrate the actual occupation of the territory under the grants. The Residents cultivate friendly relations with the natives, and by personal exploration and otherwise acquire information respecting the country, its people, and its mineral and agricultural resources. They administer justice to the natives, as far as practicable, and the natives cheerfully submit. A special flag has been adopted, which is hoisted at each station. An arrangement has been made for a steamer to keep

up communication between the several stations and
with Labuan.

At Sandakan, where the Sultan of Sooloo collected
heavy duties, amounting in some instances to more
than twenty per cent., and levied other onerous taxes
on the natives, no taxes are at present collected
on behalf of the Association, except five per cent.
duty on imports. At Tampassuk, where the Sultan
of Sooloo's rule was almost nominal, and the people
had latterly not paid any taxes, none are at
present collected. At Pappar, Kimanis, and Benoni,
on which the Brunei chiefs had a firm hold, and
where they exercised oppressive rule, custom dues of
five per cent. on imports are collected.

VI.

The Company contemplate the introduction here-
after of the system of farming out (but for purposes
of revenue only) the right to sell spirits, opium, or
other commodities, under strict regulations and superintendence, in accordance with the practice of the
Colonial Governments of Singapore, Hong Kong, and
Labuan, and with that of the Government of the
territory of Sarawak. They do not seek to secure any
general monopoly of trade for themselves to the
exclusion of any other party. Interchange of goods
and wares of every description between natives and

foreigners will be free to all comers alike, subject to customs dues. The natives will be placed on a footing of equality with European and other foreign settlers, as regards treatment in courts of justice. No foreigner, whether European, Chinese, or other, will be allowed to own slaves of any kind. The system of domestic servitude now existing among the tribes of the coast and interior will be discouraged and, as far as possible, abolished by degrees. The natives will be protected in respect of religion and property. Cases affecting their domestic institutions, such as marriage and divorce, will be determined with due regard to their laws and customs.

The Treaty of 1847 between the Queen and the Sultan of Borneo (Brunei) stipulates (Article 3) that British subjects shall be permitted to purchase, rent, or occupy, or in any other legal way to acquire all kinds of property within the dominions of the Sultan. The same treaty (Article 10), after a confirmation by the Sultan of his cession of Labuan to her Majesty, stipulates that the Sultan shall not make any similar cession, either of an island or of any settlement on the mainland, in any part of his dominions, to any other nation (that is, other than the British), or to the subjects or citizens thereof, without the consent of her Majesty. As between them and her Majesty's Government, the action of the

c

Company is justified by Article 3, and is not condemned by Article 10 of the treaty.

With respect to the British colony of Labuan, any fear that it will be injuriously affected, in trade or otherwise, by the establishment on the mainland now contemplated, is, in the opinion of the Company, groundless. Labuan, which is situated near the entrance of the Brunei River, has its principal trade with the town of Brunei, and the mainland provinces in the immediate neighbourhood, extending north to the Kimanis River and Gaya Bay, and south to the frontier of Sarawak. This trade is carried on by native boats, the imports being mainly sago, beeswax, gutta-percha, indiarubber, and other natural products, which are bought by the Chinese and other traders at Labuan, and sent on to Singapore for resale there. The exports from Labuan consist of British manufactures and other goods, given in exchange for the above-mentioned commodities. There is little trade with the mainland districts, beyond the limits above described. Occasionally, smaller vessels of European build or native craft, arrive from Sarawak, Marudu Bay, or the East Coast, but the value represented by this wider trade must be small. Besides the trade with the near mainland, a British steamer of moderate size runs regularly between Labuan, Sandakan, and the Island of Sooloo, taking out English goods of various descriptions, and bringing back native products, collected by traders, which are transhipped at Labuan to another British steamer, and taken to Singapore for disposal. Two or three times a-year, a European vessel of larger size arrives at Labuan from Hong Kong, with an assortment of goods of Chinese manufacture, or rice and salt, taking back usually hardwood timber, and smaller quantities of native produce suitable to the Chinese market. This constitutes the whole trading activity of Labuan. According to the official return in 1876, the value of the imports was about £126,000, and of the exports £112,996. Indeed, instead of injury to the trade, the operations of the Company are calculated to advance the interests of Labuan, as is shown by facts. Steamships in the employment of the Association made several visits to the harbour of Labuan in the last twelve months. This is not a matter of indifference to the small trading population there. Provisions had to be purchased ; coal had to be taken in ; a considerable amount of money was spent in various ways. As the operations of the Company extend, the visits of their ships will become more frequent. The amount of coal alone which for some time must be required for steamers will probably be sufficient to constitute the Company one of the principal customers of the Labuan coal-mines. They have acquired some land

and house property in Labuan, believing that a permanent establishment and agency will eventually be necessary there, as much of their business will naturally concentrate in the nearest British colony.* This is not without importance to the island, as, with the exception of a few Government officials and some persons connected with the coal-mines, there are scarcely any European house or land owners there.

Upon these grounds the following application was submitted to her Majesty's Government. It comprises four parts :

(a) The first point relates to the government of such British subjects as may be resident in or resorting to the Company's territory. The Treaty of 1847 (in its additional article) confers on her Majesty extra-territorial jurisdiction over British subjects within the dominions of the Sultan of Brunei. What is now asked is this : that her Majesty's Government will think fit to put into exercise this jurisdiction, so that an effective system of control over British subjects within the Company's territory may be established on a well-understood legal basis. Under the treaty this extra-territorial jurisdiction may be exercised through her Majesty's Consul-general or other officer duly appointed for that purpose by her Majesty. It is therefore not necessary that the officers to exercise the jurisdiction should be consular officers. The undersigned would mention that her Majesty might be graciously pleased to appoint the Company's Residents as her officers to exercise it.

---

* The collapse of the Coal Company in 1879 has materially affected the prosperity and importance of Labuan.

The Company's Residents will be on the spot. They will not be engaged in trade on their own account; they will necessarily obtain a knowledge of the customs, opinions, and feelings of the natives with whom British subjects will come in contact; they will acquire skill in the languages, an acquaintance with which will be requisite for the proper administration of justice. If her Majesty's Government should think fit to approve of this suggestion, the Company would undertake to provide the necessary court-houses and establishments, and generally to bear all the expenses connected with the exercise of her Majesty's extra-territorial jurisdiction, as far and as long as the exercise thereof is entrusted to the Company's officials.

(b) The second point of the application is that the Company may have the countenance and protection of British consular, naval, and colonial authorities acting in Borneo and its neighbourhood.

(c) The third point is that the Company may receive the support of her Majesty's Government with respect to the control of foreigners resident in or resorting to the Company's territory; so that the Company may be relieved of any difficulties arising with foreign Governments in relation to their respective subjects or citizens.

(d) The fourth and last point of the application is that her Majesty's Government will be pleased to grant to the proposed Company a charter of incorporation and regulation.

It was set forth that such a grant would carry with it important advantages, not only for the Company but also for her Majesty's Government:

(a) The Company would obtain the benefits of incorporation, including a recognised status in law, without being fettered by the provisions of legislation relating to companies constituted merely for the purpose of gain; many of which provisions are inappropriate to the character and position of the intended Company, as, for instance, the obligation to attach the term Limited to the corporate name.

(b) On the other hand, her Majesty's Government could, in or in connection with a charter, impose terms and conditions; whereas they could have no direct opportunity of putting any check on a company constituted by self-incorporation under the general legislation

The following were expressed as the principal terms to which the Company would be ready to submit themselves in consideration of a grant of a charter:

First.   That the Company shall be British in character.

Secondly.   That the Company shall not transfer their territory or powers to any other company, body, or persons, without the previous consent of her Majesty's Government.

Thirdly.   That any difference from time to time arising between either of the Sultans, the grantors, and the Company shall be submitted to the decision of her Majesty's Government.

Fourthly.   That the Company shall not set up or grant any general monopoly of trade.

Fifthly.   That the appointment by the Company of the chief governor of their territory shall be subject to the approval of her Majesty's Government.

Sixthly.   That the appointment of the chief judicial officer acting in the Company's territory shall, as long as that officer is appointed by the Company and not directly by the Crown, be subject to the approval of her Majesty's Government.

Seventhly.   That the Company shall freely afford all facilities requisite for her Majesty's ships in the harbours of their territory.

By making such arrangements as these, her Majesty's Government would, it was urged, do much to accomplish the desire of the Queen recorded in the preamble of the Treaty of 1847, namely : "To encourage commerce between her Majesty's subjects and the subjects of the independent Prince of the Eastern Seas, and to put an end to piracies which have hitherto obstructed that commerce."

Finally, the applicant, on behalf of himself and his associates, pointed out the prospects of the Company in their relation to the national prosperity: "The natural resources of the granted territory are great. It has splendid harbours, and a good climate for the tropics. It contains extensive forests producing much hardwood timber, and there are believed to be in it valuable mineral deposits. It will afford new outlets for British trade, new markets (which are much needed) for British manufactures, and new and rich districts for the cultivation of coffee and tea, and for tropical agriculture generally. There is every prospect of a good commercial return for the British capital employed. Civilisation and order will by degrees be introduced. And the interests of the British Empire will be promoted by the establishment of British occupation in a region offering by its situation and circumstances many strategical and other public advantages."*

---

* "Should so fortunate an occurrence ever fall to the lot of Borneo —should a strong and a wise government ever be established on her

In December, 1880, her Majesty's Government informed Mr. Dent that, after a careful examination of his statement, they were disposed to recommend to the favourable consideration of the Queen the granting of a royal charter. A few months later, in order to improve the administration of the country and extend the work of development, a Provisional Company was formed to take over the vendors' interests. The Association was essentially private, but registered for convenience under the provisions of the Companies Acts, 1862 and 1880, with a nominal capital of £400,000.

The first Directors were Mr. Alfred Dent; Sir Rutherford Alcock, K.C.B.; Richard Biddulph Martin, M.P.; Rear-Admiral Mayne; and Mr. W. H. Read. These gentlemen, acting upon the previous representations made to the Government, and setting

shores; a government that will religiously respect property, and secure to industry the fruits of her labour; that will, by a wise system of laws, protect the peaceable and punish the violator of the laws of a well-organised society; that will direct their industry to useful purposes and check their propensities to violence and plunder —such a government in a short series of years would behold, as if by magic, a paradise burst from her wilds, see cultivation smile upon her jungles, and hail a vast and increasing population, blessing the hand that awoke them to life, to happiness, and to prosperity. That so felicitous a change is not the mere reverie of a glowing imagination, nor the sheer effusion of benevolence alone, is easily demonstrable."—*J. Hunt, Esq., to Sir Stamford Raffles,* 1812.

them forth afresh, petitioned the Crown in the
following terms :

"That your Majesty's petitioner, the British North Borneo Provisional Association, Limited, consists of persons who lately agreed
to join together for the temporary purposes of acting as intermediaries between your Majesty's petitioner, Alfred Dent, on the
one hand, and a Company to be incorporated (if your Majesty
should so think fit) by royal charter on the other hand, and of carrying on until the grant of such a charter the management of the affairs
arising under the grants and commissions aforesaid, and who for
convenience of common action and for limitation of liability have
incorporated themselves under the general statutes relating to
companies, that Provisional Association having for its objects as
declared by its memorandum of association (among others) the
following (that is to say):

> "To purchase from Alfred Dent his interests and powers
> in, over, and affecting territories, lands, and property in
> Borneo, and islands lying near thereto, including Labuan.
> To acquire by purchase or other lawful means other
> interests and powers in, over, or affecting the same
> territories, lands, and property, and interests and powers
> in, over, or affecting other territories, lands, and property
> in the region aforesaid. To obtain from the Crown a
> charter incorporating and regulating a Company constituted
> with the like objects as aforesaid, or other objects relating
> to any territories, lands, and property as aforesaid. To
> transfer to the Company so incorporated any interests and
> powers as aforesaid for the time being vested in the
> Association.

"That all the interests and powers of your Majesty's petitioner,
Alfred Dent, under the several grants and commissions aforesaid,
have been transferred to and are now vested in your Majesty's
petitioner, the British North Borneo Provisional Association, Limited.

"That that Association will, in accordance with the provisional
character indicated in its name, and in pursuance of the express

provisions of its articles of association, be voluntarily wound up in manner provided by statute, as soon as a sale or disposal of its territories, lands, and property to a Company to be incorporated (if your Majesty should so think fit) by royal charter has been effected, and will after payment and discharge of its debts and liabilities, and after distribution among its members of the proceeds of such sale or disposal, and of any other its assets, be dissolved.

" That your Majesty's petitioners, Sir Rutherford Alcock, Richard Biddulph Martin, Richard Charles Mayne, and William Henry Macleod Read, are, with your Majesty's petitioner, Alfred Dent, the Directors of that Association.

" That the success of the enterprise in which your Majesty's petitioners are engaged as aforesaid would be greatly advanced if it should seem fit to your Majesty to incorporate by your royal charter a Company to carry on that enterprise.

" That such a Chartered Company would render to your Majesty's dominions services of much value, and would promote the commercial prosperity of many of your Majesty's subjects.

"That your Majesty's petitioners are in a position to raise the capital requisite for the proper and effective conduct of the enterprise aforesaid, and they hereby undertake to do so on obtaining the grant of such a charter."

VII.

Upon the above grounds, and with certain other specific undertakings in regard to the just government of the country, her Majesty in council assembled has granted to the Company a royal charter of incorporation, and consented to the Company's adoption of a flag suggestive of the royal protection. The advantages of this official recognition are numerous. That it binds all concerned in the bond

of a commercial responsibility; that it enables the
Company to sue and be sued; that it brings
its transactions within the jurisdiction of English
courts of law; these are conditions that represent
guarantees of security both to colonists, natives,
traders, and investors—guarantees which cannot fail
to be appreciated by merchants, planters, and others
who are experienced in the miscellaneous commerce
of the East.

There are possibilities attending the future of the
new Colony and the new Company which are of great
national and international interest. They will be
discussed in later pages, as will also the known
vegetable and animal wealth of the country, and its
reputed treasure of gold, copper, coal, and other
minerals. The interior of North Borneo is yet almost
unknown to the white man. All kinds of strange
traditions touching its people and its natural history
have been handed down from the earliest days of
real and mythical exploration. Recent travellers who
have steamed up its rivers, traversed its forests, and
climbed its mountains are united in their praises of the
amiability of the native Dusuns, who are its chief inhabitants, and they equally agree in their impressions
of the singular loveliness of the country; its capacity
for growing coffee, rice, tobacco, and other tropical products; its wealth of native trees, gutta and others, and

the ease with which its present small trade in sago, beeswax, edible birdsnests, camphor, hides, rattans, tortoiseshell, trepang, and pearls can be extended.

The belief that the precious metals, not to mention the diamond, are plentiful in Borneo is as old as the hills.* Gold is practicably worked in Dutch Borneo and in Sarawak, but not to any great extent. Borneo diamonds are more celebrated than numerous. But

---

* "The whole of Borneo is rich in mineral productions; those which have received attention in this Residency are diamonds, gold, and iron.

"The principal diamond mines are in the district of Landak. The Arèng (conglomerati?) in which the diamonds are found, is a kind of yellowish gravelly earth, mixed with pebbles of various sizes and shapes, and is found at different depths below the surface. From fifty to sixty feet is the greatest depth to which a shaft has hitherto been sunk, and the following, it is said, are the strata which are dug through when the Arèng is at these depths : three feet black mould, seventeen yellow sandy clay, seventeen redder clay, six or seven of a tenacious slate-coloured clay mixed with stones, an equal depth of a similar clay without stones, but mixed with pebbles, and known by the name of Amper, and six or seven of a tenacious yellow clay.

"The presence of the Amper strata is considered a sure indication of a vein.

"The mines are worked by the Dayak, Malay, and Chinese. The former proceed in the following manner. A shaft barely sufficient to permit the miner to turn round in, or at most two feet in diameter, is sunk to the Arèng. This is from one to three feet in thickness, and is dug out to the extent of seven or eight feet from the sides of the shaft, under the upper strata, which sometimes is propped up; but the laziness or improvidence of the Dayak is such, that this precaution is often forgotten, the upper strata falls in, and

tradition would lead one to believe that the mineral
treasures of the island are more likely to be found in
the hitherto unexplored districts of the north than
at any other point, and there are scientific reasons
for this opinion. In succeeding chapters we will
return to the subject of diamond and gold mining.
But it may be as well to say in this place, that the

the miners miserably perish. These accidents most frequently
occur when an adjacent shaft is sunk, which is thus done: The
Arèng in the first mine being expended, and the course of the vein
ascertained, a new shaft is sunk in that direction at the distance of
fifteen or sixteen feet from the preceding, to enable the miners
when arrived at the Arèng to work back to their former mine, and
the same process is repeated until the vein be exhausted. The
Arèng is hoisted up in small baskets by bamboos, on the ends of
which part of a branch is left and forms a small hook. The search
for the diamonds is conducted in an equally simple manner. Small
dulans, circular trays slightly converging towards the centre, are
nearly filled with Arèng; and the Dayak sitting himself in the
nearest stream immerses the dulan, and works the Arèng by hand
until the earthy particles begin to separate; the dulan is then
brought to the surface, and a rotatory motion is given to it, until
the water it contains, being saturated with earthy matter, is poured
off, and this is continued till such time as the water comes away
clean. The pebbles, etc., which remain in the centre then undergo a
strict examination. . . .

"The largest diamond known with certainty to have been found in
these mines weighed thirty-six carats. It was long supposed that
the Sultan of Matan possessed one weighing three hundred and
sixty-seven, which it was said he was afraid to cut lest it should
prove flawed, but gentlemen to whom it has been lately shown consider it not to be a true stone."—"*Notices of the Indian Archipelago*,"
edited by J. H. Moor, published at Singapore, 1837.

possibility of important discoveries in that direction is
not in any respects a leading feature of the hopes and
anticipations of the modern explorers of Borneo.

VIII.

This annexation by a company of London merchants,
capitalists, and travellers of a country larger than
Ceylon, and as valuable as any known territory of
the Malay Archipelago, recalls the beginnings of more
than one of our great colonial possessions. It suggests
the early days of our Eastern Empire, but in such
shape as to lead to the hope that it marks a new era
in the history of the colonising aspirations of the
Anglo-Saxon, the era of pacific annexation, the
business alliance of whites and blacks in the cultivation and development of the neglected places of
the world.   To increase and multiply and govern
the earth seems to be a special Anglo-Saxon
mission. An instinct of possession, a general "land
hunger," is a prevailing characteristic of the race.
In the old days we sallied forth, and by right
of might added to our empire new lands for
our surplus populations. To-day, capital even more
than industry is seeking for fresh fields of enterprise. Sir Rutherford Alcock, who has taken a
friendly interest in British North Borneo for some

years, believes there are many enterprising persons
with a little capital who will turn their attention
to such a possession as this, "who have hitherto
been precluded from settling in Ceylon and other
colonies in the Indian Archipelago."*

Having introduced the reader to the newest depar-
ture, or we might better say revival, in British
enterprise, let us turn our attention to the remarkable
and little known scenes where the new power has
been so unostentatiously established.

---

* "The great want in our days seems to be some healthy place
where planting can be carried on, especially of tea, coffee, cinchona,
and all such like products of India and Ceylon. Young men are not
so willing to adopt the pen and desk as they used to be ; but are
more anxious to seek fields for tropical agriculture, or country life of
some sort. It is useless, as Sir Rutherford has pointed out, for a man
to go to Ceylon now unless he has a capital of £5000 at least in his
pocket, as the good forest-land is selling there at from £18 to £25 per
acre. It is moreover stated that there are not more than 30,000 to
40,000 acres of land left in Ceylon and suited for the cultivation of
coffee arabica, or other produce of the hills, at an elevation of over
2000 feet. We think this want is supplied in North Borneo, and
that in respect of climate, soil, rainfall, labour, and disposition of the
natives, it affords a better field for the young planter than Perak or
Johore, where experiments are now going on."—*Mr. Alfred Dent, at
a Meeting to discuss the affairs of North Borneo, March* 26, 1879.

LANDS OF PERPETUAL SUMMER.

The Island of Borneo—Sarawak and the Dutch Possessions—Interesting Statistics—Travellers' Tales—Native Women—Strange and barbarous Customs—Human Sacrifice—A previous Age of Civilisation and Prosperity—Mineral Treasures—Gold Mines—Famous Diamonds.

I.

"FRAGMENTS of a continent," although now "a geographical unit," is Wallace's description of the Malay Archipelago. In prehistoric ages Asia and Australia were united. This was in what geologists call the Secondary Epoch. "The processes of subsidence and upheaval resulting in the present insular formations were not, however, developed till a much later period."

Glance at your map and take note of the extent of these fragments, one of which is considerably larger than England. They have been not inaptly called "The Gardens of the Sun." Chief of these "isles of the sea," lands of perpetual summer, is Borneo. Situated on a great ocean highway of trade and commerce, possessing noble harbours, and rich in all kinds of tropical products, it is, with the exception of Australia, the largest island in the world. It is 850 English miles in length, its greatest breadth 600. Its coast line is upwards of 3000 miles; its area is 280,000 statute square miles; it is larger than France, and more than three times the size of England. It is bounded on the north by the Sooloo Ocean, on the east by the Straits of Macassar, on the south by the Java, and on the west by the China Seas.

The English have always been sensible of the value of Borneo, commercially and otherwise. As early as 1706 they made efforts to establish themselves on its coasts. The only appearance of success in the history of these attempts was the occupation of a small island on the north, which was eventually abandoned. Various reasons are alleged for the failure of the English authorities; probably their secured possessions in other parts of the East sufficiently occupied their time and attention. The Spaniards and the Dutch were their competitors for supremacy in the Malay Archipelago, and these maritime powers succeeded in planting their flags upon many of the rich, though comparatively unknown, islands of the Eastern Seas.

Until forty years ago the story of Borneo was that of an uncivilised country, the possession of which was a bone of contention between the Dutch and the English. Oliver Van Noort visited the island in 1598.

D

A few years later his countrymen began to trade with it. In 1609 they concluded a commercial treaty with the rulers of the Sambas, and built a factory. After about twenty years of effort they abandoned the idea of establishing a settlement.

In 1707 the English appear on the Bornean coast. They build factories, but with no permanent success. In 1763 they take possession of Balambangan, and in 1775 the garrison is successfully assaulted by pirates. A year later the Dutch establish a factory at Pontianak, and in 1780 the reigning powers cede part of the west coast to the Dutch. In alliance with the Sultan of Pontianak, they destroy Succadana, and in 1787 are granted portions of the south coast. In 1812 an English expedition goes out against Sambas and fails; to succeed, however, in 1813. In 1818 the Dutch, who during this war had been expelled by the English, return, and their Bornean colonies are now formed into a special government.

Sir James Brooke visited Borneo in 1839, to succeed in carrying out, by his own personal energy, what the great East India Company had failed to accomplish. He founded Sarawak. With the aid of Admiral Keppel he annihilated the dangerous hordes of pirates that infested the western coasts. He successfully stamped out a rising of

Chinese, in which operation the native tribes loyally came to his assistance; and he has demonstrated, financially and politically, the wisdom of those early Dutch and British adventurers who saw a splendid property in the island of Borneo. In 1847 the English Government, seeing the importance of a station in this latitude, purchased Labuan, an island off the coast of Borneo, and made it an English colony, with a governor and all the necessary officers and appliances of an efficient administration. Such is the brief history of Borneo, possession of which is now divided between the Dutch Government, the Sultan of Brunei, Rajah Brooke, and the British North Borneo Company, the latter recently endorsed in its undertaking by the royal charter of her Majesty Queen Victoria.

II.

Borneo has been made familiar to the general reader by the settlement of Sarawak, which is situated on the western side of the island. Rajah Brooke's territory consists of over 30,000 square miles. The justice of its administration has enhanced the character of the white man throughout the island, and has done much towards establishing the perfect confidence reposed in Englishmen wherever they may present themselves among the natives from shore to shore.

Alone and unaided, without state protection or official service, for forty years Sarawak has maintained an independent position, her English chief holding sovereign power, his government being often spoken of by travellers who have visited Borneo as an example worthy to be studied by some of the world's greatest powers. The British North Borneo Company have raised their flag over about the same extent of country as that which comprises Sarawak; and they have wisely imitated the policy of Rajah Brooke in ruling the natives through their chiefs, and with all due respect to their own laws, customs, and religion. Sarawak is a happy and prosperous colony. With a population of 240,000 souls, it has a respectable military force, garrisons, and forts; it pays a competent staff of European and native officers; and maintains three gunboats to protect its commerce and guarantee the safety of life and property to its subjects.*

---

* "The history of the English Rajahs of Sarawak is well worthy of study by politicians and statesmen; and it opens up the great question of whether the future of the human race might not be benefited by the extension of the system here inaugurated, of the free government of small semi-barbarous states, under trained and educated English gentlemen, untrammelled by the cramping influence of official subordination, and unburthened by the dead weight of a complex governmental organisation and an elaborate system of legal and official precedents. What finer field can we imagine for the energies of young men of talent and fortune, than thus taking part in the raising of depressed races, the formation of free states

In 1871 the imports to Sarawak amounted to 1,427,923 dollars, and the exports to 1,268,337 dollars; while in 1879 the imports were 1,938,964 dollars, and the exports 1,980,290 dollars. In 1871 the revenue returns were 157,501 dollars, and in 1879, 229,302 dollars. The expenditure in the latter year was 191,629 dollars, leaving a surplus of 37,673 dollars. The Dutch claim suzerainty over all the other portions of Borneo that are not occupied by Rajah Brooke in Sarawak, the British North Borneo Company in Sabah and the Sultanate of Brunei. They have established something like a regular government over the coast districts of the west and south. They have Residents in the southern and eastern districts, and their chief town is Pontianak. A native sultan is nominal ruler. They have as yet however done nothing in the way of developing this colony compared with their working of other possessions, notably the neighbouring island of Java,* the

and the advancement of civilisation? And what more admirable means can be suggested of elevating such races, than the being placed under the rule of men whose one object would be to save them from oppression, misrule, and social misery, to educate them to self-government, and so enable them to grow unfettered to whatever degree of civilisation they are capable of attaining?"—"Australasia," by A. R. Wallace.

* "The rule of the Dutch in this fine island is very successful. Good roads traverse it in every direction, life and property are as safe as in any part of Europe, and the inhabitants are as happy and

exports from which amount to about twelve millions sterling, the net revenue remitted to Holland (previous to the Acheen war) varying from two to four million pounds sterling.

contented as any people are likely to be under the rule of an alien race. The system by which the people have been made to work at fixed wages, and to sell certain products at fixed rates to the Government, has enabled the Dutch officials to remit a large annual revenue to Europe; but this has been done without any serious oppression of the natives, who have always been accustomed so to work for their native chiefs, or on the lands of the village community. One of the best tests of the general well-being of a community is that of the growth of the population; for where this is steadily increasing, where there is no pauperism, where serious crime is rare, and where famine and rebellion on any important scale are almost unknown, the government cannot be otherwise than suitable to the people governed. This is the case with Java. In 1850 the population was about 9½ millions, in 1865 it had increased to close upon 14 millions, in 1874 it was 16½ millions, and at the present time it is estimated at about 18 millions. It has therefore nearly doubled in eighteen years, and, notwithstanding that a large portion of the surface of the island is covered with lofty mountains and trackless forests, it supports a population of greater density than Great Britain. There are about 30,000 Europeans in Java, and 156,000 Chinese. The army consists of 27,000 men, of whom 11,000 are Europeans. . . . It may safely be predicted that if the Dutch Government freely throw open Java to the world, the result will be that many capitalists will make fortunes, but the native inhabitants will not be benefited. The exports from Java amount in value to ten or twelve millions sterling annually; and the net revenue which is remitted every year to Holland varies from two to four millions."—*Wallace.*

III.

Notwithstanding the suzerainty of the Dutch in one district, and the efficient government of Rajah Brooke in another, the interior of Borneo and the northern regions have been until quite recently a *terra incognita*. The home of the orang-outang, tradition gives to this country a race of wild people living in trees, and tribes of savages who occupy themselves chiefly in extending their trophies of skulls. Coupled with these horrors, travellers have declared the country to be rich in diamonds and gold, a sort of combined Golgotha and Golconda. Even to-day the Dutch possessions in Borneo would seem to be almost "an unknown quantity," judging from the latest work on the subject, issued under the title of "The Head Hunters of Borneo," written by Carl Bock, the publisher's announcement stating that: "The author gives an account of his overland journey in Borneo, as leader of the Dutch Government Exploring Expedition. Among other matters, the book describes and gives drawings of the fair-skinned race inhabiting the forests of the island, of whom the women at least have never previously been seen by any European traveller." I have letters before me from travellers now exploring North Borneo, who are

the first white men to make the acquaintance of many
of the native tribes; but at present they have come
upon no *lusus naturæ*, or degenerate man, such as
Dr. Maclay met with in Johore, or such as previous
travellers declare they have seen in Borneo. For
example, the *Singapore Chronicle*, of 1831, contained
the following notes, written by Mr. Dalton, who had
resided on the east coast of Borneo. They are reprinted
in Mr. Moor's "Notices of the Indian Archipelago:"

"Farther towards the north of Borneo are to be found men living
absolutely in a state of nature, who neither cultivate the ground
nor live in huts; who neither eat rice nor salt, and who do not
associate with each other, but rove about some woods like wild
beasts. The sexes meet in the jungle, or the man carries away a
woman from some kampong. When the children are old enough to
shift for themselves they usually separate, neither one afterwards
thinking of the other; at night they sleep under some large tree,
the branches of which hang low. On these they fasten the children
in a kind of swing; around the tree they make a fire to keep off the
wild beasts and snakes; they cover themselves with a piece of bark,
and in this also they wrap their children; it is soft and warm, but
will not keep out the rain. These poor creatures are looked on and
treated by the Dayaks as wild beasts; hunting-parties of twenty-five
and thirty go out and amuse themselves with shooting at the children
in the trees with sumpits, the same as monkeys, from which they are
not easily distinguished. The men taken in these excursions are
invariably killed, the women commonly spared, if young. It is
somewhat remarkable that the children of these wild Dayaks cannot
be sufficiently tamed to be entrusted with their liberty. Selgie (the
Dayak chief of Coti) told me he never recollected an instance when
they did not escape to the jungle the very first opportunity,
notwithstanding many of them had been treated kindly for
years."

Mr. George Windsor Earl, author of "The Native Races of the Indian Archipelago," and "Eastern Seas," in his former work, published in 1853, discounts this information. He desires the reader not to forget that it is obtained from natives, who having organised parties for hunting these singular beings, were interested in making them appear as much as possible in the light of wild beasts.

IV.

There are as many versions of the appearance and character of the native women as there are types and races. It is well known that some of the Malay women are attractive, and, from a Mongolian point of view, even beautiful. The Milanos of Borneo are one of the most numerous of the tribes. Mr. W. M. Crocker, an administrator as well as traveller in Sarawak, says the Milano women have won a reputation for beauty; but while there are a few good-looking girls among them as a tribe, they are behind the Malays in figure and regularity of features. They are very white (*i.e.* an unhealthy milky white), and their heads are flattened in childhood. Their work of treading or expressing the sago makes their feet very large, and their figures are squat and stumpy. Mr. Crocker

believes the practice of flattening the heads of
children in Borneo is entirely confined to the Milanos.
"I have not heard," he says, "of its having been
found to exist among any of the numerous tribes
which inhabit the Eastern Archipelago. A similar
custom prevails among the Indians of the Mosquito
shore." Mr. F. W. Burbidge, who was in Borneo
during the year 1878, on a naturalist's expedition,
is eloquent as to the graces of the women he saw
at Kambatuan, a village of British North Borneo.

"We had a large concourse of the villagers in to see us this evening
after dinner, including 'Beuhan,' the headman, who wears a head-
cloth and kriss, and in general build and physiognomy resembles the
Sulus much more than either Dusun or Malays. 'Kurow' was the
principal talker, and related all that we had done and how much
he had helped us in ascending the mountain. The young girls
crowded to see us, and tried hard to get speech with us. We had
given the girls who brought us fruit a looking-glass each, and we could
quite well understand that all were eager for a similar gift. They
were very, very scantily clad; indeed the most tolerant of Lord
Chamberlains might well wish to add an inch or two to their tiny
petticoat, especially as 'tis the only garment of which they can
boast. It answers somewhat to the American definition of a dress
'which began too late and left off too soon.' Here, however, it is
the customary fashion, and as such is honoured. How graceful were
the figures of some of these young girls! Perfect little Amazons,
lithe of limb and having regular features, eyes full of gentle ex-
pression, and a richness of raven hair most European ladies might
envy. It is pleasant to know that these dusky girls, lovely as some
of them are, will never be degraded to anything worse than field
labour, which is a far better lot than that of their Malayan sisters
along the coast, whose personal charms chance to be interesting.

We found out later on in the evening that the pretty damsel who had first brought us fruit was the headman's daughter, 'Sa' Tira' by name. Most of the evening she knelt by the fire, her dainty little fingers busily making cigarettes for her papa's guests, many of whom had arrived from other villages near to look at us. Altogether we spent a very pleasant evening with these hospitable people, and we have no doubt but that they will long look back to our visit themselves, seeing that whole months frequently elapse without their seeing anyone from the coast even, much less a white man or two from far-off Labuan."

"The Journal of the Indian Archipelago" for 1849 contains some interesting notes by Mr. Burns, "the first European," says the editor, "who has ventured to explore the interior of Borneo Proper." Speaking of the Káyáns, he says the sexes are in about equal number; that they enjoy the social intercourse of civilised people; that unchastity is of rare occurrence; that marriage takes place at an early age; that adultery is punished with death, so also is theft, while murder is a matter of compromise with "the parties concerned." The Káyáns are a proud race. The men as a rule do not tattoo, but many of the higher classes have small figures of stars, beasts, or birds on various parts of their bodies, the highest mark of distinction being the colouring of the backs of the hands, which is only conferred upon the brave in battle. With the women, the arms, from the elbows to the points of the fingers, are beautifully tattooed, as are also the legs from the thighs to a little below the knees, and likewise the upper parts of the feet; and those of very high rank have in addition one or more small spots on the breasts. In tattooing the performer pricks the design or pattern with three needles, and afterwards smokes it with a dammar torch, by which process a beautiful dark-blue is produced; but inflammation of a serious nature frequently follows. The operation of tattooing begins when girls are about four or five years of age, and is continued gradually, the latest ornamentation being finished at woman-hood. With both sexes while very young, the lobes of the ears are perforated, and large rings of copper, brass, or tin inserted, by which that part of the organ is extended commonly from five to seven inches, but frequently more. In women especially, it is considered a mark of beauty to have them extended to the breasts, which is quite common among them. As the loss of her flowing locks to a European belle, so to a Káyán beauty would be the deforming or breaking of her pendant ear-lobes. The earrings are commonly in weight about twenty ounces each pair.

The traveller came upon no evidences of canni-balism, and the natives whom he saw indignantly repudiated the suggestions of such barbarism. "But," he says, "it would seem to have been pre-valent amongst them formerly, especially on the occasion of the king or principal chief taking possession of a newly-built house, and also on the occasion of his death." An instance of this revolting custom was acknowledged to have taken place about two years previously, when Batu Dian entered upon his new abode. "The victim was a Malay slave girl brought from the coast for the avowed purpose, and sold to the chief by a man who was also a Malay. It is said to be contrary to the Káyán custom to sell or sacrifice one of their own nation. In the case alluded to, the unfortunate victim was bled to death, the blood was taken and sprinkled on the pillars and under the house, but the body was thrown into the river. It is the blood only that is prized, or considered efficacious. During my stay in the house of the chief Knipa Batu, one of his children, a little boy, was at the point of death from fever. After exhausting all their skill in applying remedies, as a last resource the chief took a young chicken and passed it a number of times over the face of the child, then with his most valued war sword killed it at the window, and threw it upwards from him in the direction of the setting sun. The sword with the blood on it he then held over the face of the child as before, with fervent invocation, desiring that his beloved child might not die, and laying himself down beside the unconscious little sufferer, indulged in the wildest paroxysm of grief."

Many other strange and barbarous customs are mentioned by travellers in the olden days. Some of their narratives may be taken with a grain of salt. Several recent visitors to Borneo, especially in the north, seem only to have found regions of Arcadian simplicity.*

v.

It is curious that the barbarism described by early travellers should have had, according to tradition and history, a previous period of something akin to commercial prosperity and civilisation. In an official statement made by Mr. J. Hunt to Sir Stamford Raffles in 1812, he says that "when the Portuguese first visited Borneo, in 1520, the whole island was in a

---

* "A voyage of a few weeks brings us to these beauty-spots of the Eastern Seas—to an 'always-afternoon' kind of climate—where winter is unknown. Warmed by perpetual sunshine, deluged by copious rains, and thrilled by electricity, they are really enormous conservatories of beautiful vegetation—great Zoological Gardens inhabited by rare birds and curious animals. In these sunny garden scenes man is the Adam of a modern Eden. Primitive in habits and numerically insignificant, he has scarcely begun his battle with things inanimate, or his struggle for existence as it is known to us. At home we have man as in some sort the master of Nature, but in the Bornean forests Nature still reigns supreme. Here with us man wrests his sustenance from her—there she is lavish in the bestowal of gifts unsought."—*Preface to " Gardens of the Sun,"* 1880.

most flourishing state. The numbers of Chinese that had settled on her shores were immense; the products of their industry, and an extensive commerce with China in junks, gave her land and cities a far different aspect from her dreary appearance at this day, and their princes and courts exhibited a splendour and displayed a magnificence which has long since vanished." This is borne out by Pigofetta, who spoke of the town of Brunei having 25,000 houses and being "rich and populous." Later accounts describe the frequent visits of Chinese and Japanese junks to the Bornean ports. In 1809, however, there were not 3000 houses nor 6000 Chinese in the place, and up to that time (nor since, I believe) a junk had not for years been seen in Bornean waters. "But," says Mr. Hunt, "the ports of Borneo have not dwindled away more than Acheen, Johore, Malacca, Bantan, Ternate, etc. All these places likewise cut a splendid figure in the eyes of our first navigators, and have since equally shared a proportionate obscurity."

Mr. Hunt attributes the cause of this remarkable change to a decay in commerce. "In exact proportion as the intercourse with the Europeans with China has increased, in precise ratio has the decrease of their direct trade in junks become apparent. The Portuguese first, and subsequently the Dutch, mistress of the Eastern Seas, exacted, by treaties and other ways, the Malay produce at their own rates, and were consequently enabled to undersell the junks in China. But these powers went further; by settling at ports on Borneo, or by their guardes de costas, they compelled the ports of Borneo to send their produce, calculated for the China market, to Malacca and Batavia, which at length completely cut up the direct trade by means of the Chinese junks." The loss of direct intercourse with China compelled the adoption of a circuitous course which doubled the cost of carriage, and finally destroyed the trade. Not only did this throw labourers out of employment, it stopped the emigration of the Chinese, whose industry and mechanical skill had enhanced the local prosperity. The rajahs, finding their revenue reduced, turned their attention from trade and commerce to maritime and piratical enterprise. Agriculture was thus neglected, and lands hitherto profitably cultivated were allowed to run to jungle and to waste.

VI.

The fertility of Borneo in the matter of vegetation is a favourite theme of all travellers, ancient and modern; and without the same established and easily accessible proofs to back their statements, they are all agreed as to its enormous mineral wealth. In the past, exaggerated reports were published by travellers who excited the imaginations of their readers with descriptions of Borneo diamonds and Borneo gold. According to some of these romances, it would seem as if these precious treasures were lying about, await-ing the arrival of venturous explorers to pick them up. It is true that dangers were suggested, some of them not inferior to the monstrous guardians which watch over the treasures in "The Arabian Nights." But with all this smoke there was a certain amount of fire. When Mr. Hunt was in Borneo, there were gold mines in the vicinity of Sambas and also at Matan. Mention of this latter district recalls the subject of " the largest known diamond in the world," the reality of which is doubted by several writers and travellers. Mr. Edwin R. Streeter, in his recent work on "Precious Stones and Gems," however, considers the history of this diamond to be sufficiently established for record as a genuine stone. Models of it exist, and many travellers have seen it. Several battles have been waged for its permanent possession, and it is said that the Governor of Batavia offered 150,000 dollars and two ships of war for it. The Rajah, in declining the offer, is reported to have replied that he would not part with it on any terms, believing that it is a talisman upon the possession of which depends his happiness and that of his family.

E

Of more genuine interest than a crystal representation of this questionable diamond, were some fine specimens of Bornean pearls, imported during the present year from the North Borneo Seas, which Mr. Streeter showed me. One of these is still to be seen at Bond Street, in its original condition, attached to the shell; another has gone to Messrs. Tiffany, of New York. The favourite pearl fisheries of the ancients were in the Persian Gulf, the Indian Ocean, the Red Sea, and on the Coromandel coast. The Phœnicians traded with Ceylon for pearls. In 1640 the Dutch seized the Ceylon fisheries, and in 1798 the English, having come into possession of the island, obtained in one year a profit of £140,000 on the fishery. This success was, however, the result of giving the beds a long rest. The yearly harvest of pearls is estimated at £350,000. The merchants engaged in the trade are chiefly Indian, Arabian, and Persian. The pearls found in the Persian Seas are sent by way of Muscat to Bombay, and on to China, "which adds to its stores many pearls from the Sooloo Archipelago, lying between Borneo and Mindanao." Philip IV. of Spain had a pearl weighing 160 carats. It came from India, and is now in the possession of Princess Youssopoff, and its value to-day is £16,000. The Shah of Persia's famous pearl, more than an inch in diameter, is valued at £64,000, and the Sultan of

Muscat has one worth £32,000. Within the past few years many valuable pearls have been "in the market." A very fine white pearl was sold in London a few years ago for £2600. It weighed 116 grains. In 1878 another was imported weighing 114 grains, and, like the first-mentioned, of a peculiarly brilliant sheen. They were on view at the Paris Exhibition, and are now in the possession of the Baroness Alphonse Rothschild. "No European regalia contain such a pair; they are thought to be unique." To students of Bornean gems, there is a far more interesting treasure on view, at Mr. Gordon's place of business in Bond Street, than the pear-shaped model of the Rajah diamond. This is a genuine stone, which was purchased from a Chinaman about four years ago by the Rajah of Sarawak. Found at Landak, it weighs 70 carats, and is of the purest water. This exquisite gem is known as "The Star of Sarawak." The tradition of Borneo as a diamond region, and the non-scientific character of some of the explorers, occasionally lead to serious disappointment. Recently a traveller shipped to England a stone which was to eclipse in splendour some of the most notable of known diamonds. It was pronounced by several amateur mineralogists to be a genuine diamond. The finder entered into a bargain with a certain traveller for its sale. Having insured

it for £4000, they committed it to the care of the
Peninsular and Oriental Company, who delivered it
safely to a trusted friend in London. Submitted to
an expert, the verdict was, " A pebble of no value."
The doubt which rests upon the Rajah stone lies
chiefly in the fact that the owner will not have it cut :
and there is much reason to fear that it must be
relegated to companionship with "the Braganza" of
the Portuguese state jewels which remains in the
rough, a reputed diamond of 1680 carats, the value
of which, if genuine, might be set down at over
£58,000,000 sterling.

Mr. Crocker, a former Resident of Sarawak, whom
I have previously quoted, read a paper at the Royal
Geographical Society in February, 1881, in which he
stated that the upper country of Borneo is rich in
minerals, that gold is still worked by the Chinese,
and diamonds* by the Malays. In Sarawak all their

* "From the slovenly manner in which the diamonds are sought
for by the Dayaks, they seldom collect them of a size exceeding
three or four carats weight each. When rough, the Landa diamond
has a white or yellow hue; but none are found of that inky and
flinty tinge so valuable in some of the Golconda diamonds. But that
Landa does produce them of a very considerable size, the extensive
and valuable specimens in Java, as well as the quantities annually
sent to Batavia, will evince. The King of Matan is at this instant
in possession of a diamond weighing 367 carats, the value of which,
according to the old mode of calculation, would be $367 \times 367 \times 2 =$
£269,378. The Sultan of Pontianak says, however, that a much

minerals are leased to a company whose exports of antimony and quicksilver are thus set forth in their trade returns: "Antimony exported from 1859 to 1879, 25,000 tons, value more than one million dollars. Quicksilver exported from 1870 to 1879, 15,000 flasks, value 717,500 dollars." Gambier and pepper are being cultivated with great success, and there is every prospect of a large influx of Chinese capitalists and coolies. Experiments have also been made from time to time in cultivating coffee, sugar, and tapioca.

In an elaborate report on the distribution of the useful minerals in Sarawak, made in 1874 by Mr. A. Hart Everett, late Resident of Bintulu, Sarawak, and now an officer of the British North Borneo Company, he discredits somewhat the traditional belief in the vast deposits of the precious metals.*

larger price was offered for it by the Dutch Government of Java. He refused, it is said, twenty-five laks of dollars, two sloops of rice, fifty pieces of cannon, and a hundred muskets. Several from twenty to thirty carats have been dug up. At Mompava there are said to be very rich copper mines; but from want of population, a vigorous government, and scientific mineralogists, little is to be hoped from them at the present day. At Pulo Bongorong, near Borneo Proper, there is plenty of loadstone found."—*J. Hunt, Esq., to Sir Stamford Raffles*, 1812.

* Formerly, if the labours of the miners were rewarded by success, which is very uncertain, stones under four carats were their property; all of that size and upwards were claimed by the

"It has been the office of time," he says, to dissipate "the golden fancies" which have always more or less existed in connection with the island of Borneo. "Nevertheless," he adds, "there does

Panambaham, then a tributary of Bantam, from the Sultan, of which State the former Dutch Company purchased this monopoly or royalty, for 50,000 dollars. At present, by treaty with the Panam-baham, all the stones must be delivered to Government at twenty per cent. below the market price which is ascertained by appraise-ment on the spot, the necessary advances being of course first made to miners by Government. The small stones are sold at Pontianak, and the large ones, for which there are no purchasers there, are disposed of at Batavia, and the profits equally divided between Government and the Panambaham. There is every reason to believe that in the first year and a half succeeding this arrangement, which was made in the middle of 1823, these amounted to about 19,000 guldens, 390 carats having been delivered to the agents of Government in the latter part of 1823, and 1900 in 1824, the cost of which must have been 33,000 guldens, and the proceeds 52,000. The existing regulations are no doubt as often evaded as that mentioned above must have been, and if such be the case, 2290 carats are less than the actual produce of the period in question. The number of persons employed during it is unknown, so that no idea can be formed of the profit on mining speculations. The deliveries of 1825 and 1826 were less than that of 1824, and will be still less this year, Government not advancing to an equal extent, in consequence partly of an outstanding balance against the miners, and partly to the disinclination of the latter to receive copper money. Some natives are of opinion that the veins are not so productive as in former times; others, making due allowance for the decrease occasioned by the measures of Government, say that they are not worked with equal zeal.

Gold is found in almost every part of the Residency, also in the Arèng strata, and takes many names, being invariably designated by

exist a certain amount of solid foundation for the idea that Borneo is well furnished with the useful metals and minerals." Upon the subject of "the mineral resources of Borneo as a whole," he describes some of the leading geological features of the island, and gives instances of gold, coal, diamonds, iron, and cinnabar, being found not only in, but beyond the limits of Rajah Brooke's territory. "Gold," he says, "occurs in the form of fine sand or minute flattened plates in alluvial deposits over a great part of Sarawak." Washings are carried on in various districts by Chinese and Malays, but in a very inefficient and superficial way. Nuggets are of

the name of the place where it is procured. The gold of Sintang, Sangâo, and Landak, are about nine touch; of Muntuhari about eight and a half, that of Mandor a shade below eight; these are places under Pontianak. That found at Mantradu under Mampawa is about eight touch; and under Sambas, gold of nine touch is found; at Sapan of eight; and eight and a half at Larak; of eight at Siminis; and of seven and a half at Salakao. The mines are worked in a similiar manner to those already described, and the Arùng cleaned in the dulan, in the centre of which the gold, from its greater gravity, is collected. There are no data for ascertaining the amount produced, or the number of persons employed. The price at the principal ports may be taken at about two dollars and ninety cents per touch; or say, twenty-six Spanish dollars for Sintang gold of nine touch. The Sultan of Sambas has in his possession a lump weighing twelve-and-a-half bunkals, and says he has seen some which weighed twenty-five.—*Notes on " Residency of the North-west Coast of Borneo," in Singapore Chronicle, October 6th, and November*, 1827.

rare occurrence, but "if the Chinese are to be
credited, some of very considerable weight have been
met with in the adjacent Sambas district." As to
the annual produce of gold in the territory of Sarawak,
the data for making an approximate calculation of the
total amount produced is unreliable. " Mr. Low, of
Labuan—whose work, in spite of its being somewhat
out of date, is the most trustworthy yet written on
Sarawak—places the yearly export of gold from the
territory at 7000 ounces. Although nominally all
gold carried out of the country must be declared, as
much leaves Sarawak in a private way as is declared
to the export office in Kuching, while a still more
considerable portion of annual output is bought up
and remains in the country without in any way
showing in the trade returns." On the whole, the
opinion of Mr. Everett seems to be that whatever
minerals may be awaiting discovery in Sarawak,
" their importance can only be relative or comparative
with that of the coal-fields of North-west Borneo.

III.

BRITISH NORTH BORNEO OR SABAH.

Geographical Situation—Harbours in which the British Fleet can
ride at anchor—Mountains and Rivers—Village Life and Local
Agriculture—Soils and Climate—Trade and Barter—Tropical
Products—Anglo-Bornean Homes and Gardens—Fruits and
Flowers—Crocodile Stories—Opportunities of Sport—Elephants
and Rhinoceros—Familiar and Curious Fish—The Sun-bird—
Pearls and Pearl Fisheries—A Dramatic Story—The Natives—
Cessation of Piracy.

I.

A ROUGH line drawn across the map from the Kimanis
River on the north-west coast to the Sibuco River
on the east coast, will indicate the territory hitherto
called Sabah, now to be better known in the future as
British North Borneo. This territorial possession is
in shape that of an irregular triangle, two sides of
it washed by the sea, the apex going out into the
ocean in picturesque splendour. A coast-line of
more than 500 miles in extent, every part of the
country has a seaboard, the commercial advantage of
which need not be dwelt upon. No other territory

in Borneo is so favourably placed either on the score
of climate, facilities of trade, or in regard to the
possibilities of development. Situated nearly midway
between Singapore and Hong Kong, it is in immediate
proximity to the Palawan Passage, which is a great
ocean route for vessels trading to China and Japan.

The finest harbours in all the coasts of Borneo
are Gaya Bay, Ambong, and Abai-Usukan Bay on
the west; Kudat on the north, and Sandakan Harbours
on the east coast. They are indicated in the map
accompanying these brief historic notes, and are also
shown in detail on separate charts.

Gaya Bay will bear comparison with any harbour
in the China Seas. Having one entrance capable of
easy defence, and with accessible coal beds, its
commanding position gives it special strategical importance. The entire fleet of Great Britain might
ride at anchor in its deep and extensive waters. It is
more than probable that the British authorities have
taken note of this important fact. Sandakan, having
like Gaya Bay an entrance that especially lends itself
to easy defence, is a sheet of deep water, fifteen miles
long by five miles broad. It has many excellent
anchorages that afford perfect shelter in either mon-
soon for the largest ships. The Admiralty have
published a chart of this harbour, and there is no
doubt that Sandakan will eventually become the

great rendezvous of trade of the Sooloo and New Guinea Seas, as well as a place of call for vessels bound to and from Australia.

No more remarkable example of the unexplored character of the country can well be mentioned than the fact that one of its finest harbours has only just been discovered. Commander Johnstone, of H.M.S. *Egeria*, sent home the first notification of the existence of Kudat in August, 1881, and it now appears for the first time on the Admiralty chart. The Governor of the new territory, Mr. Treacher, with Mr. Everett and Mr. Witti, visited it on the 25th of August in the Company's launch *Enterprise*, and it has been decided to establish a Residency in Marudu Bay, overlooking the newly-discovered harbour. "Anyone entering Kudat," says a despatch dated August 29th, 1881, "cannot fail to be struck with the commodiousness of the harbour, and the eligibility of the site selected for the future town. I am assured that there is ·6 of a square mile of deep-water anchorage, that is, with a depth of not under five fathoms at low water. Scarcely any clearing will be required on the proposed town site for some time, and there will therefore be probably less sickness to contend with at first than is usually to be expected on opening a new station. Water will be obtained by means of wells as at Labuan and Alai.

Mr. Everett, in his report on harbours, has reported highly in favour of Kudat. A harbour on the mainland has many advantages over one on a detached island, since, in addition to the transit trade it attracts, there is that of the country at its back to help to swell its returns of imports and exports. In the case of Kudat this will in all probability be of considerable importance, for Mr. Witti states the country to abound in gutta-percha, indiarubber, ebony, etc., and he seems to have little doubt from the information he has obtained from natives, that coal exists in Marudu Bay. He also states that there is a large and tractable Dusun population. Sir Stamford Raffles has recorded his opinion to the effect that any settlement by Europeans on an island off Borneo would be a failure, and he recommended Marudu Bay as the best locality for a European settlement. Mr. Everett remarks: 'Kudat is so situated that it would inevitably come, in time, to intercept all the trade from Palawan, Balabac, Cagayan Sulu, and Sulu, that now passes westward through the Malawali passage,' and he thinks it possible that much of the trade of the Southern Philippines may find its way hither in course of time."

The other geographical features of British North Borneo are no less interesting and important than these, which include grand natural bays, alike valuable as trading stations and harbours of refuge. The country is traversed by a mountain range averaging from 5000 to 8000 feet in height, and rising to the noble altitude of 13,700 feet, crowned in lofty grandeur by Kina Balu, deemed by the natives sacred, as are the heights of Mount Shasta by the American Indians in California, and Fusiyama in Japan. Many picturesque spurs branch off from this mountainous backbone of the country, terminating in rich undulating hills, watered by stream and torrent, diversified by plain and forest, rich in tropical verdure, and presenting many possibilities of mineral treasures; besides adding to the advantages of agricultural and other operations in a hot country the cooling breezes of high lands, that go down in rush of torrent and rocky majesty to the open seas. Among the many rivers of British North Borneo are the Paitan, Sugut, Sibuco, and Kinabatangan. The latter forms a perfect waterway from the east coast into the heart of the country, and can be navigated for 200 miles with small steamers.

The spurs and slopes of Kina Balu are peculiarly fitted for growing coffee, tea, and cinchona; while the rich plains that mark the course of the Kinabatangan and other rivers lend themselves to the culture of indigo, tobacco, cotton, rice, and the other well-known tropical products. Such villages as the traveller meets with

on excursions in the interior are fed and maintained
by agriculture, the successful features of which belong
to the natural fertility of the soil rather than to the
science of the native farmer.　Take for example the
little village of Tamparulie on the banks of the
Tawaran.　*En route* from Labuan to make the ascent
of the Kina Balu mountains, you pass this native
hamlet.　You cross a plain of rice, bananas, cocoanut-
trees, and other luxuriant vegetation.　You see the
native cultivator at work, his rude plough drawn by
buffaloes, flocks of white padi birds sailing aloft,
or a few solitary cranes adding an oriental touch to
the picture.　You halt on the river-bank amidst
tropical groves, here and there relieved by neatly-kept
gardens fenced down to the water's edge, and containing plentiful supplies of sweet potatoes, cucumbers,
maize, and kaladi.　Farther on, at Kolawat (a native
village backed by a grove of plumed palms, the betel-
nut variety, yellow with fruit) you will find a village
built on poles in a morass, with herds of swine and
flocks of tame bees as part of the local treasures.

Along the valleys that go upwards to the hills you
pass straggling huts and bamboo cottages surrounded
by irrigated patches of rice, with maize and sweet
potatoes growing nearest the houses, and in many
cases clumps of bananas at the very doorways.　Now
and then you meet natives laden with baskets of

tobacco and beeswax going towards the coast on
trading expeditions; the gentle manners of the
people, their means and mode of life, being charac-
terised by great simplicity. While you thus at
intervals come upon evidences of village life and
agricultural work, you may travel hundreds of miles
without any other signs of life than those belonging
to "the forest primeval," Nature's splendid legacy of
fertile soil and umbrageous woods being literally given
over to the orang-outang and other strange examples of
animal life. You may steam along the Kinabatangan
River for a hundred miles at a stretch without seeing
a human being, though all the time you are passing
through a country presenting unrivalled opportunities
for the cultivation of rice, sago, sugar-cane, tobacco,
pepper, and other tropical merchandise. Face to face
with these scenes of "luxurious nature," the European
traveller cannot fail to regret that such "lands
of plenty" have remained so long unavailable for the
stimulating exercise of capital and labour and the
useful arts of civilisation.

II.

Authoritative reports, surveys by experts, and
scientific analyses of soils demonstrate beyond dispute that British North Borneo offers advantages to
planters and colonists not surpassed by the most

favoured and popular countries of the tropics. Experienced and observant travellers have indeed spoken of it as "The New Ceylon." *

It will be interesting to set forth somewhat in detail the vegetable productions of commercial value which are indigenous to the soil and growing wild in the forests. Indiarubber and gutta-percha abound in great plenty, the latter trees growing to the height of nearly a hundred feet and being upwards of six feet round the trunk. The natives do a small trade in these commodities with Labuan and other merchants. The Gonzogin people prefer in exchange for this produce brass of any shape or kind, while, as a rule, coloured cloths, salt, and pottery are the favourite

---

* "After weighing the advantages and disadvantages of opening a coffee estate at Pappar, I would not advise anyone to commence operations at Gallamuttai, but, as all Ceylon planters know, our best districts are not twenty miles as the crow flies from our worst, and the resemblance to Ceylon in the lie of the land, appearance of the jungle, soil, rainfall, temperature, climate, and degree of latitude, is so striking, that looking round in the jungle it is difficult to fancy yourself out of the Central or some parts of the Southern Province of that island. I therefore feel certain that valleys along the range can be found far superior to the valley of the Gallamuttai in soil and lie of the land which would grow good coffee and would pay. The difficulties I have mentioned of commencing planting in Borneo are precisely the same as those which planters met with in commencing in Ceylon (except the weakness of the government), and would soon be overcome. The Company will, I am sure, give every assistance towards getting labour and supplies, but pioneers in Borneo would have the great advantages of being able to choose

material of barter. The camphor-tree is found in many parts of the country. Barus camphor (a different species from the ordinary camphor of commerce) is highly valued by the Chinese for its medicinal properties, and is readily purchased by them at fifteen dollars per pound. The middlemen, or traders dealing with the natives by exchange, find a good profit in completing their sales for current coin. Along the entire east coast is an immense virgin forest. The woods are of infinite variety, suitable for every purpose of carpentry, building, or ornamental work, the most noteworthy being ebony, mallape, puon (for spars), and the bilian wood. The contiguity of rivers that run out to the great natural harbours of the country make it certain that British North Borneo can easily

good land and leave the bad, as, if they were Ceylon planters, they could tell one from the other, which the pioneers in Ceylon could not do, as they had no practical experience of coffee, and many of them learnt to their cost that it did not always follow that where fine jungle stood good coffee would follow. I have confined my remarks to Coffea Arabica, but I cannot conclude without stating that all along the banks of the Pappar River, and in some of the jungle at low elevations, i.e. up to 200 feet, I found the soil very rich-looking, and I believe the climate is suitable for Liberian coffee (which, however, is still hardly out of its experimental stage in the East), pepper, nutmegs, cocoa, sago, sugar, rice, tapioca, tobacco, in fact all products that flourish in the Malayan Archipelago."—*Report on North Borneo, by T. S. Dobree, Esq., of Ceylon, made on behalf of several Ceylon merchants and planters, October, 1878.*

F

compete for the large and growing demand of China and Japan for timber of any description.

The articles in regular cultivation by the natives are rice, millet, tapioca, Indian corn, sugar-cane, tobacco, cotton, pepper, and several kinds of tropical vegetables. Sugar-cane attains in some districts to an extraordinary height and thickness. It is mostly grown for immediate consumption. While one tribe of natives crush their cane, another use it in the shape of molasses, calling it "paha," the name they give to honey. Cotton is grown in the interior, and samples of it show a long fine staple. It is not yet an article of export, the natives manufacturing it in a primitive way into yarn for their own limited use. The women also make a rough cloth from the fibre of the "lambra," a broad-leaved weed that is often seen growing in or near the scattered villages. Other curious textile fabrics are produced from the bark of a tree having leaves something like the bread-fruit. There are several localities where tobacco is grown, notably near the Ananam River in Gaya Bay, and, as in the case of cotton, it is sufficiently good to give full assurance of the adaptability of the climate and soil for the successful establishment of tobacco and cotton plantations; while land and labour for the erection and working of factories are procurable on terms that could not fail to encourage and nurture any suitable

industry. Reliable travellers say that nowhere
could pepper and rice grow more luxuriantly. The
sago palm is the basis of a fair native trade, the
product finding a ready market at Labuan and Singapore. Cassia lignea is also exported. Cocoa-nuts,
the areca palm (yielding the betel-nut), together with
pretty well every variety of fruit known in the tropics,
such as mangoes, limes, oranges, bananas, and pine-
apples, are found in many parts of the country.
Rattans are met with in especial abundance near the
river-banks on the north-east coast. They are superior
to those of other countries, and ought to represent a
very profitable trade in China, as well as in the
European markets.

III.

While not regarding British North Borneo from
the standpoint of a settlement for Europeans, except
on the lines of a tropical colony, there are evidently
spots among the Bornean hills where the tropical
heats are so modified by mountain air that it would
be not difficult to establish comfortable and pleasant
Anglo-Bornean residences, with gardens combining
familiar English vegetables and fruits with those
of Eastern celebrity. Mr. Spenser St. John found at
the village of Kiau that the thermometer never

marked above 77° during the day, and varied from
66° to 69° during the nights. The Marei Parei spur
of the Bornean mountains he regarded as offering a
fine position for a sanitarium at any height between
4000 and 5000 feet. In a tent pitched at about
4700 feet the thermometer registered 75° (mean) in the
midday shade, 56° at 6 A.M., and 63° (mean) at 6 P.M.
This, he says, would be a delightful climate in a well-
built house. The day will no doubt come when
prosperous villages will be found in these salubrious
regions. Returning to the passing fancy of our
English house with its horticultural surroundings, it
is worth while to mention that the garden stuffs of
British North Borneo already include onions, garlic,
pumpkins, beans, greens, and cucumbers. Mr. St.
John says turnips, cabbage, and potatoes would also
succeed if there were Europeans to attend to them.
The sweet potato is indigenous to the country,
and think of the fruits an English gardener could
grow without glass! Mr. Burbidge, who is a great
botanical authority, says the pine-apple of South
America, the mango of India, the delicious little
Chinese or mandarin orange, flourish here in the open
air, yielding two crops in twelve months, while most
of the other fruits may be obtained all the year round ;
the forests of Borneo being the native home of the
mangosteen, durian, tarippe, langsat, rambutan, and

jintawan.* A land of perpetual summer, the home of all that is beautiful in tropical life, its hills and dales radiant with rare plants and flowers, its glades and forests rich in the finest fruits of the earth, it is a happy thought of the latest student of its botanical and zoological treasures to collect and publish his notes under the suggestive title of "The Gardens of the Sun."

IV.

The animal productions of the country are both interesting and valuable. The natives carry on a considerable trade in that luxury of the Chinese, edible birdsnests. They are found in large quantities near the Kinabatangan River and neighbouring provinces, and also in other localities. They sell in

* Apart from mere commercial estimation, except in so far as beauty of vegetation has a trade value, British North Borneo is a natural botanical garden, in which the rarest examples of tropical life that are treasures at imperial Kew are the common plants and flowers of the country. The giant pitcher-plant of Kina Balu was discovered in 1881 by Mr. Low, her Majesty's Resident in Perak, and with its allies is illustrated by Sir Joseph Hooker in the transactions of the Linnæan Society. These strange plants, the search for which and the efforts to cultivate in European countries have occupied so much attention on the part of botanists, are only known to exist at Kina Balu. The list of Bornean ferns set forth by Mr. J. G. Barker is an interesting chapter in "The Journal of Botany."

China, according to quality, at from 40 dollars for common black to 3000 dollars per picul for the finest white kinds.

Beeswax is plentiful, the product of bees both tame and wild. A great trade might be done in hides and horns of cattle and deer. On a recent trip up the Kinabatangan River, Mr. W. B. Pryer, the Company's Resident at Sandakan, noticed that everywhere along the bank the tracks of buffaloes, deer, and pigs were so abundant as to form perfect roads. A fine breed of cattle, far superior to any in China, Saigon, Siam, or the Straits, is found largely distributed along the north-west coast, and might be utilised as an article of export. At Pinowautei, during one of his recent excursions, Mr. Witti found herds of buffaloes. They are reared in this locality, he was informed, only for local food. While Mr. Witti mentions these cattle grazing on what may be called flat meadows, Mr. Pryer speaks about the old deserted clearings near Blut and Seebongan as having fine glades of rich grass, in which places deer, buffaloes, and pigs are abundant, the grass often being eaten quite short, and in some places almost "puddled up" by cattle tracks. There is an almost total absence of beasts of prey, the feline species being represented by a small cheetah in the interior of the island. The crocodile is found in most of

the rivers, and various reports are current as to
its character. Most travellers are careful to offer
a note of warning against "promiscuous bathing;"
but Mr. Witti, during quite a recent excursion,
says of the crocodiles that infest the Tandek River
that they are just as tame as those of the Bengkoka
are fierce. In the former river people bathe,
literally " keeping company " with these formidable
reptiles. He learnt, however, on the river-shore
south of Tamalan, that the crocodiles thereabouts
carry off dogs, pigs, and occasionally natives.
Mr. Pryer, referring to his investigations on the
Kinabatangan River, says the crocodile is really a
dangerous creature. It rarely ascends the river above
Blut, not liking the shallows, but in the neighbourhood
of Seebongan it is large and fierce, and has been
known to attack large canoes. Hardly a month
passes in which a native is not carried off. Mr.
Pryer saw a crocodile hereabouts of enormous size.
In these days, when crocodile hide has become
popular for boots, portmanteaus, dressing-cases, and
other articles, sport in the Bornean rivers might be
combined with considerable profit.

Elephants are numerous in the Company's territory
of Sabah. A magnificent tusk was recently sent
home to Mr. Dent by one of the Residents. In a
letter from Mr. Pryer, from Elopura (Sandakan), dated

November 22nd, 1879, he says: "Should there be a shooting yacht at Singapore (as I hear there is), the following bag, by Torrie and his party, will interest them: Four elephants, a stag, and a bison, and lots of elephants let off. This is close to the coast; so that the shooting-party need never sleep away from the steamer." In another recent letter he says: "I have an elephant's head here. Ibrahim, with four men, sallied out while three elephants were destroying their paddy. Ibrahim had his gun half filled with powder. Two of the elephants (tuskless) ran off, but the third faced about. Ibrahim blazed away, blew up his gun, was knocked down and stunned; but he had sent a ball right into the brute's skull. The elephant charged right and left, nevertheless, right at the prostrate Ibrahim; but the other four men fired a volley and killed it. The brute stood nine feet seven inches, and his tusks are thirty-two inches in length."

The two-horned rhinoceros shares portions of the country with numerous kinds of deer and wild cattle. The orang-outang is, however, the most noted "denizen of the woods;" but he has never been known to betray any of the savagery of Du Chaillu's gorillas. The Bornean "wild man" is quite harmless. Mr. Wallace has hunted him, shot him, and, capturing him alive, has tried to train him; but as yet no one has succeeded in pushing the Darwinian theory into the practical illustration of an educated ape or even a useful one.* Old Bornean travellers, however, as we have seen, profess to have discovered a sort of degenerate man, who is possibly accepted by some philosophers as the missing link.

There are snakes of various kinds in all parts of the island, but death from their bite is almost unknown. The most formidable reptile Mr. Burbidge saw during

* "The Malays of Samarinda catch the orangs near the small creeks and streams falling into the Mahakham near the town. They told me that the animals only come to the banks early in the morning, returning during the day to the jungle. When they catch one alive they sell it for three dollars to the Chinese, who feed the animals first on fruit and afterwards on rice, but never succeed in inducing them to live long in confinement. The captive animals seem capable of little or no activity, sitting for an hour or longer in the same position, so still that they could be photographed with the greatest ease, then slowly turning on one side and sleeping with the arm under the head. Their eyes are very keen, and give them a very intellectual and human-like appearance. The remarkable listlessness of the orangs in captivity made me extremely anxious to see them in their native woods and jungles, but I was never fortunate enough to see a single orang-utan alive or dead in any part of the interior, though the Dayaks of Long Wai said they were found farther north and on the Teweh; I also heard that they were by no means rare in the Doesoen district, where they are called 'kooe.' It is only among the Malays that they are known as orang-utan (literally 'wild men'). Dr. Solomon Müller, in his 'Travels,' says the natives have distinct names for the sexes; the male being called 'Salamping,' and the female 'Bookoe.' "—"_The Head-Hunters of Borneo_," _by Carl Bock_ (1881).

his travels was a sea-snake. The Hon. W. H.
Treacher, the Governor, took him on an excursion
from Labuan, and, near the Bornean shore at daybreak, the native boatmen "pointed to a large sea-
snake, lying full-length on the surface of the water
in the sun. It was about eight feet long, and of a
blue-black colour, barred with rich golden-yellow,
the belly being dull white. Mr. Treacher fired at it
with a shot-gun, striking it about the centre of its
body; and we could see quite plainly where the shot
had ripped its skin. As it lay quite motionless for
several seconds after the shot we inferred it to be
dead; but on the men paddling the boat towards it,
it dived quite suddenly, and, as the water was clear
and still, we could distinguish it at a great depth
below the surface." Several travellers in these
regions have mentioned to me the wonderful clearness
of the sea at various points, and also of the rivers,
reminding one of the startling and unique examples
of this kind which you meet with in the mountain
lakes of California, where, sailing in a boat, you seem
to be floating in space.

v.

Fish are plentiful and of many varieties. Recently,
while lying off the entrance to more than one of
the rivers, her Majesty's gunboat *Lapwing* was

plentifully supplied from "the continual harvest
of the seas." Among the fish most relished were
herrings and mackerel; not exactly like our own,
but sufficiently similar to be eminently satisfactory.
Opportunities of a large dried-fish trade with China
present themselves at several points of the coast.
Fresh-water fish are also abundant, and there are
travellers who have enjoyed sport with rod and line in
Bornean rivers that would have contented the most
ardent followers of Izaak Walton. Trout are not only
found in the streams, but with the British instinct of
striking at flies. It is no exaggeration of terms to say
that both land and water in Borneo present remarkable
sporting attractions, as have indeed been exemplified
by sketches sent home to the editor of *The Field*.
The natives, while rowing you about on sea or river,
usually run out a line at the stern of the boat, just
as one does in the waters of the Upper Thames. The
results are a little different. A monster of formidable
growth is often the captive in the former case; a
Thames jack of a dozen pounds is not so bad as the
trophy of a long quiet pull above Henley.

But while you are fishing in the waters of "The
New Ceylon" your gun need not be idle. The
avifauna of Borneo is particularly rich. The famous
pheasants of China are not more beautiful than those
of Sabah, and its hornbills are said to be gigantic

compared with those of South America. There are
many kinds of pigeons; paroquets are common and
various; the oriole, one of the showiest of tropical birds,
is seen here to perfection; a remarkable blackbird is
common by the rivers, but more plentiful is a kingfisher
of gorgeous plumage. Padi-birds, curlew, sandpipers,
crows, eagles, ospreys, owls, bats, flying foxes, and a
hundred other examples of winged creation are to be
found in the hills and forests, on the plains and by
the rivers, including the sun-bird, which may be
called the humming-bird of the tropics. They are
described as being ethereal, gay, and sprightly in
their movements, flitting briskly from flower to flower,
and assuming a thousand lovely and agreeable atti-
tudes. As the sunbeams glitter on their bodies, they
sparkle like so many precious stones, and exhibit at
every turn a variety of bright and evanescent hues.
As they hover round the honey-laden blossoms, they
vibrate their tiny pinions so rapidly as to cause a
slight whirring sound, but not so loud as the humming
noise produced by the true humming-birds. Occasionally they may be seen clinging by their feet and
tail, busily engaged in rifling the blossoms of the trees.
They appear to be as common in Borneo as they are
in Ceylon, where they are familiar in the gardens. They
thrust their slender beaks into the flowers, and supple-
ment "the nectar of flora" with dainty meals off

small insects and spiders. Sir James Emerson
Tennent says of them: "If two happened to come
to the same flower—and from their numbers this has
often occurred—a battle always ensued, which ended
in the vanquished bird retreating from the spot with
shrill piping cries, while the conqueror would take up
his position upon a flower or stem, and swinging his
little body to and fro, till his coat of burnished steel
gleamed and glistened in the sun, pour out his song of
triumph."

VI.

In addition to other products, the sea yields mother-
o'-pearl shells, seed pearls, bêche-de-mer or trepang, and
tortoise shells ; and beyond these treasures pearls are
a feature of Bornean trade, and the fisheries which
have made Sooloo pearls famous are on the north-east
coast. Mr. St. John, in his "Life in the Forests of
the Far East," says, while there are pearl-banks in
the neighbourhood of Brunei and Labuan, the most
remarkable are those found in the Sooloo seas, where
they are more numerous than in any part of the
world, and, "if properly developed, would, no doubt,
be exceedingly productive." The new rulers of North
Borneo or Sabah will, of course, see to this. At
present the natives are content to dredge for them in
a very primitive way, and in comparatively shallow

water they will dive for them, but not where there is anything like a depth of eight fathoms. "I heard," says Mr. St. John, "of an Englishman endeavouring to send down men with a regular diving-helmet, but it was said he found that the current was so strong as to prevent the air passing down the tubes by flattening them; but there must have been some mismanagement." Occasionally there are magnificent pearls taken to Labuan for sale. Mr. St. John heard of a remarkably fine one, and well shaped, which was purchased by the Hon. George Edwards, late governor of Labuan, "and was pronounced by all who saw it in the East as the best that had been brought under their notice. I have seen very handsome ones myself, some perfectly round, others slightly pear-shaped." A friend of mine recently brought several fine specimens from Borneo, and as previously intimated, specimens are to be seen in Bond Street, and no doubt at the place of business of any of the great London dealers in gems and precious stones. Mr. St. John relates the following dramatic incident of the fisheries:

"The natives tell a story of a certain chief, who was a great trader, and fond of sailing a prahu from Sulu to Manilla. During the course of his voyages, he made the acquaintance of an English merchant, who had, on various occasions, trusted him with goods and treated him very liberally, not an unusual circumstance in the East. At last the chief took to gambling, and squandered all his property, sold his houses, his slaves, and at last lost a large sum and was obliged to place his wife and children in pawn as security. The only property he had preserved was a favourite slave-boy, and with him he started in a small canoe to the oyster-banks. There they remained fishing, and had varied success, but every day increasing the amount in the hollow bamboo in which the natives generally keep their small seed pearls. In the evenings the chief would talk over the tales they had heard from other fishermen, who delighted to recount the story of the vast pearl which was seen by the men of old, and actually brought in its oyster into a canoe, but had slipped from the fingers of the incautious captor. The natives declare that the oysters containing the largest pearls are always open, until you approach them, and that by cautiously peering into the water they may be seen.

"One day the slave-boy was preparing to dive, when he started back, touched his master's sleeve, and with signs of great emotion pointed into the water; he could not speak. The chief looked, and there, seven fathoms below them, lay an oyster, with an enormous pearl distinctly visible. Without a moment's reflection he plunged in, and dived with such skill and speed that he reached the shell before it closed, and actually had his fingers caught in it. He thrust hand and shell into his bosom, and, being an expert swimmer, rose quickly to the surface, and was helped into the boat by his anxious follower. They then forced open the oyster, and there lay a pearl, unsurpassed in size, and of an extraordinary shape. They pulled back to Sugh, and selling all his smaller pearls, the chief redeemed his wife and children, and set sail for Manilla. There he went to the house of his English friend and said: 'Take this pearl, clear off my debt, give me what you like in return, I shall be satisfied.' The merchant took the pearl, gave him what he considered its value, at all events, enough to make Sulu ring with his generosity, and sent the pearl to China, but what became of it afterwards I could never distinctly trace, but I learned that a pearl in Bengal, which was called there the 'Mermaid,' originally came from China; and as the one found in Sulu was said to be shaped like a woman's bust, it is probably the same."

It is a general superstition throughout the far East,

that if you place pearls in a packet by themselves
they will gradually decrease in number until they finally
disappear, but that if you add to them a few grains
of rice the treasure is safe.   The same belief holds as
to gold.   In the case of pearls the rice is even supposed
to increase their number.

VII.

British North Borneo is at present but thinly populated. In the provinces of Kimanis, Benoni, and Pappar,
on the north-west coast and as far as Gaya Bay, the
inhabitants of the villages on the rivers and near the
seashore are principally of Malay origin, intermixed
with a few Bajus and descendants of the natives of
neighbouring islands.   From the Mengkabong River,
on the west coast above Gaya Bay, as far as Marudu
Bay in the north, all the villages near the sea are
inhabited by Bajus and Llanuns, the latter having
originally come from the island of Magindanao, the
southernmost of the Philippine group.   From Marudu
Bay, in a southerly direction along the seashore of the
east coast, and as far as Cape Unsang, but few villages
are met with, and these are principally inhabited by
natives from the Sooloo Islands or Bajus, interspersed with a few traders of Indian, Chinese, or
Arabic origin.   All these different races profess the
Mahometan religion.

The interior of the country is inhabited by the descendants of the aboriginal population, called variously Muruts, Dusuns, or Ida'an, and corresponding in their external appearance in many respects to the Dayaks of Sarawak and the southern parts of Borneo, although the colour of their skin is much lighter than that of any other natives in the island, owing possibly to the large admixture of Chinese blood in former centuries, when the northern part of Borneo is said to have been largely inhabited by Chinese colonists. The Ida'an are by nature peaceful and docile, and by habit essentially agriculturists. They raise rice, sweet potatoes, yams, Indian corn, sugar-cane, tapioca, tobacco, and cotton, though the latter only in certain districts, and the former only sufficient for their own consumption, and for procuring in the way of barter such articles of foreign manufacture as they require to supply their simple wants. They are the only natives of the country known to use a plough, and this of very primitive construction. Here and there agricultural implements of a rough kind are used; and, as nothing of the sort is found in the south of Borneo, they are no doubt remnants of that Chinese civilisation which is alluded to in the earlier pages of the present work. There can be no doubt that under the new rulers the Chinese will soon be tempted back again to contribute

their labours and ingenuity towards the development
of this long-neglected land of sun and flowers.

Says Mr. St. John : " I first saw the natives ploughing in the Tampassuk ; their plough is very simple,
and is constructed entirely of wood ; it serves rather
to scratch the land than really to turn it over. The
plough was drawn by a buffalo, and its action was
the same as if a pointed stick had been dragged
through the land to the depth of about four inches.
After ploughing, they use a rough harrow. In the
Tawaran they ploughed better, the earth being
partially turned over to the depth of about six
inches. The Ida'an have divided the land into square
fields with narrow banks between them, and each
division being as much private property as English
land, is considered very valuable, and the banks are
made to keep in the water. Their crops are said
to be very plentiful." These natives use a bamboo
sledge drawn by buffaloes to take their goods to
market. They supply their own district with tobacco. They are of settled habits, and their villages
peaceful.

It is estimated that the native population in Sabah
counts up about 150,000. Piracy in former times was
rife along the coast of Borneo, and many of the
most dreaded piratical tribes of the Eastern Seas had
their fortified strongholds there, causing the island

to be shunned and avoided by the navigators of earlier days. All this is now changed since Admiral Sir Thomas Cochrane, with the British fleet under his command, bombarded and took the town of Brunei, and destroyed the powerful piratical settlements on the Tampassuk and Pandassan Rivers, and in Marudu Bay; and since Captain (now Admiral) Sir Henry Keppel, in H.M.'s ships *Dido* and *Mœander*, assisted by Sir James Brooke, performed similar and equally efficient service against the fleets of sea rovers infesting the seaboard of Sarawak and the southern part of Borneo Proper.* Ever since that time the piratical fleets of former days have entirely disappeared. Practically speaking, piracy has ceased to exist on the north-west coast, while on the east coast occasional piratical attacks by Sooloo or Balignini pirates on native coasting craft are still reported, although they are not of very frequent occurrence. Steamers and European sailing vessels navigate those seas in perfect safety, and it may be asserted without exaggeration that more piracies are committed at the present day on the much-frequented coast of China, in the immediate vicinity of British settlements, than in the isolated waters of Borneo.

* For a graphic and complete description of the operations of H.M.S. *Dido*, see Admiral Sir Henry Keppel's "Expedition to Borneo," two vols. (Chapman and Hall).

IV.

STRANGERS AMONG STRANGE PEOPLE.

Recent Expeditions and Discoveries in Sabah—Forest and Stream—
A Novel Mode of Travel—From Pappar to Konquot—Mr. Dobree
on Coffee-planting—Hunting the Rhinoceros—Slavery—Mr.
Witti's Overland Journey from Marudu Bay to Pappar—Dis-
covery of a New Oil—Dusun Girls in Danger—Singular Toilettes—
Native Weapons—Head-hunting—Buffaloes—The First White
Men in Tambuan—Notes on the Pappar River—Geographical
Fables—Native Canards—Men and Women with Tails—English
and other Maritime Powers in the Eastern Seas—Present and
Future of the Indian Archipelago—European Capital and
Chinese Labour.

I.

IF Borneo* is a " strange and unknown land," Sabah,
the territory of the British North Borneo Company,
is the least explored portion of this remarkable
island. For nearly two centuries it has remained a geographical mystery, a fabled treasure-house, a region

---

* " Borneo and Celebes, and indeed the greater portion of the
islands of the Malayan Archipelago, are still unknown, and the
apathy of two centuries still reigns supreme with the enlightened
people of England ; whilst they willingly make the most expensive
efforts favourable to science, commerce, or Christianity in other
quarters, the locality which eminently combines these three objects

of tropical wonders, the paradise of botanists, a realm
of strange and traditional romance. Even the natives
of other parts of Borneo, notably at Sarawak, regard

is alone neglected and alone uncared for. It has unfortunately been
the fate of our Indian possessions to have laboured under the prejudice and contempt of a large portion of the well-bred community.
Whilst the folly of fashion requires an acquaintance with the deserts
of Africa, and a most ardent thirst for a knowledge of the usages of
Timbuctoo, it at the same time justifies the most profound ignorance
of all matters concerned with the government and geography of our
vast acquisitions in Hindostan. The Indian Archipelago has fully
shared this neglect ; and even the tender philanthropy of the present
day, which originates such multifarious schemes for the amelioration
of doubtful evils, which shudders at the prolongation of apprentice-
ship for a single year in the West, is blind to the existence of slavery
in its worst and most aggravated form in the East. Not a single
prospectus is spread abroad, not a single voice is upraised to relieve
the darkness of Paganism and the horrors of the eastern slave trade.
Whilst the trumpet-tongue of many an orator excites thousands to
the rational and charitable objects of converting the Jews and re-
claiming the gipsies ; whilst the admirable exertions of missionary
enterprise in the Ausonian climes of the South Sea have invested
them with worldly power as well as religious influence ; whilst we
admire the torrent of devotional and philosophical exertion, we cannot help deploring that the zeal and attention of the leaders of these
charitable crusades have never been directed to the countries under
consideration. These unhappy countries have failed to rouse attention
or excite commiseration ; and as they sink lower and lower, they afford
a striking proof how civilisation may be dashed, and how the purest
and richest lands under the sun may be degraded and brutalised by a
continued course of oppression and misrule. It is under these circumstances that I have considered individual exertion may be use-
fully applied to rouse the zeal of slumbering philanthropy, and to
lead the way to an increased knowledge of the Indian Archipelago."—
Rajah Brooke, in Keppel's " Expedition to Borneo."

the unfamiliar districts of the north with awe and superstition. They have on several occasions assembled to gaze with admiration upon pioneers and explorers setting out for the countries that lie in the splendid shadows of Kina Balu.

It is only within the past few years and under the auspices of the Company that Sabah has been explored at any distance from the coast. In the year 1878, Mr. T. S. Dobree, a distinguished planter of Ceylon, visited the new cession of North Borneo on behalf of several planters and merchants connected with Ceylon, for the purpose of ascertaining if the land is suitable for the cultivation of coffee. His report is eminently favourable. I propose to strip it as much as possible of mere technicalities, and deal with those portions which are most likely to interest the general reader. There can be nothing more interesting in the way of travel than the first impressions of an explorer in a new country; while the ancient books of our first adventurers who sailed through unmapped seas to equally unrecorded countries are amongst our most fascinating literature. The diaries of Stanley, Speke, Grant, Burton, and other modern travellers have the special charm of a current realism. They deal with men and things that are known to exist to-day, with countries which are open to our own personal investigation as they were to

theirs; and their narratives are not open to that
suspicion of "over-colour" which belongs to some of
those early histories which criticism has relegated to
the literary company of romances under the cynical
title of "Travellers' Tales."

The reports and letters which I propose to examine
and discuss with the reader were not prepared for
publication. They are semi-official documents, written
chiefly for the edification of business men. Nevertheless, here and there we shall come upon incidents
and episodes of travel which are of peculiar interest.
As plain statements of fact they have a special value
of their own. Mr. Dobree travelled through the
forest lands on the banks of the Rivers Galamuti and
Leemai, situated thirty-five miles south of Pappar
village, which, with the other points mentioned in
this and previous chapters, will be found duly marked
in the accompanying maps. He found the Pappar
River lined with cocoa-nuts and roughly-cultivated
patches of sugar-cane, hill-paddy, mango, plantain,
and other products. He began his journey up the
river on the 23rd of June, and was on the banks of
the Galamuti on the 28th. Two days later he sent
off the baggage in a canoe to Pappar, and started with
Tahatan, his guide, on buffaloes, as he wanted to see
the land away from the banks of the river. He does
not recommend this as a comfortable way of travelling,

but he says it is better than walking if you are going anywhere on the plains where a canoe is not available. The buffalo path cuts off the bends of the river, but crosses several tributaries, which the buffaloes have to swim, and until you have learnt to stand on the animal's back while it is swimming (as his guide did) a buffalo mount is not pleasant. It is nevertheless much better than swimming yourself, and marching constantly for a mile at a time through swamps. They arrived at Pappar very stiff and wet, the canoe having got there about an hour earlier. All the land Mr. Dobree rode through was more or less cultivated, and was said to be private property, chiefly belonging to the Dusuns, who live in the country lying between Pappar and the hills, and do all the cultivation. The Malays live in Pappar, and are a thoroughly lazy, worthless set, their accomplishments loafing and paddling canoes. They trade a little with Brunei, and make a little cocoa-nut oil, but burn the fibre.

Pappar village is a group of about twenty houses, all built on piles of the nibong palm, bamboo walls, and roofed with cadjans made of nipa palm-leaves; the floors are also of split nibongs. The headman would give no assistance to the expedition. The Dusuns, on the other hand, were attentive, and rendered all the aid they could. From Pappar to Nygapass (with the exception of the build of the

houses and the language of the people) the surroundings of scenery and vegetation are so similar to that
of parts of the southern province of Ceylon, especially
about Ginganga, that Mr. Dobree found it difficult to
fancy himself anywhere else.

From Pappar to Konquot (the place where Mr.
Dobree commenced his march) it would be extremely
difficult to construct a road that would be always
passable, on account of the swampy nature of the
ground, but the river is navigable and would be
sufficient for all purposes. From Konquot to the
hills a good road could easily be made along the
bank of the Galamuti without any necessity for cross-
ing the river once.

"From what I heard in Singapore and Hong Kong, I feel quite
confident that any number of Chinese coolies might be had for
about fourteen rupees a-month, who would in a short time work as
well as or better than our Tamil coolies. There would of course be
trouble and expense in starting this, but no real difficulty. Chinese
would have to be imported for curing and shipping the coffee at
Pappar, as I don't believe the inhabitants of that village would do
anything. Chinese shops and banks would follow as soon as their
necessity arose. All rice, and food of every kind, would have to be
imported, also all requisites for estate purposes. The rice would
come from Saigon at Rs. 2.50 a-bushel, other things from Singapore."

After commending the country as a good field for
coffee-planting, and dwelling upon its various advantages in the matter of land at a nominal rent, easy
means of transport, and the plentiful supply of labour

to be had from China, Mr. Dobree mentions districts which he considers suitable for coffea arabica and also for Liberian coffee. Between Pappar and Benoni he says there is an enormous swampy forest of about 8000 acres, all available and suitable for sago; and security for life and property being established, he says British North Borneo is "a splendid field for tropical agriculture."

II.

In his report on Sandakan Bay and the country round the harbour and up the Kinabatangan and Se-Gally Hood Rivers, Mr. Dobree says: "Sandakan Harbour is on the north-east corner of Borneo, and is about forty-eight hours' steam from Labuan. It is fifteen miles long and about five broad in the widest part, perfectly sheltered from all winds, and with plenty of water for the largest ships. The land all round the harbour is one dense forest, extending right up to Kina Balu on the north-east, and as far as the eye can reach on the west, south-east, and south. On the north side of the harbour the land is steep, rising to 600 feet in three hills near the mouth, in which coal has been found. On the south side it is flat, with rolling hills up to the height of about 200 feet. The forest, which is magnificent, especially on the south side, comes down to the water's edge, where there is a fringe of mangroves. There are three small native villages in the bay, German, Timbang, and Oopak; the largest, German, has about sixteen houses, all built on piles in the water, cadjan walls and roof. The inhabitants live on fish, with which the bay abounds, and rice, which they get by exchanging for beeswax, trepang (or sea-slug), birdsnests, shark-fins, seed pearls, gum damer, gutta, camphor, and rattans. The harbour abounds with fish." On the Se-Gally Hood River, which he reached about the middle of July, 1878, he found numerous tracks of elephants.

" On the 28th I went out below the village on the right bank, and about two miles from the clearing found the fresh track of a rhinoceros, which I followed up, and, coming on him in about a mile, killed in a mud hole. I also saw a bear to-day, and tracks of wild cattle and pig; the jungle was the same as I went through the day before, magnificent, and the soil rich and deep. I saw some camphor trees, and enormous mallapu and tappan trees; from the latter the natives generally get the honeycomb; the former, which is commonly eighteen feet in circumference above the roots, and 150 feet to the branches, is used for canoes and planks. If a market could be found for this timber, any amount might be procured and cheaply floated down to the harbour."

Slavery exists in some part of the country. While Mr. Dobree was at Sandakan early in 1878, three prahus came in with slaves for sale from the Sooloo groups of islands; the slaves were in a wretched state of starvation, and several died of dysentery. One that died at Oopak was taken on shore, and the natives practised with their krises on the dead body. On the whole, however, he thinks the slaves are very well treated while alive. They look as well fed and dressed as their masters. The poor creatures brought into the prahus had been suffering from a famine at Sooloo before they were caught.

III.

Mr. Dobree reported on the country about Tampassuk and Pandassau and the valley of the Ginambau. After a brief geographical sketch of the first-mentioned river, he says that recently he went to see one of the finest sugar estates in the Straits Settlements, and from what he saw there, he believes the soil at Tampassuk to be finer than that of the Straits, while the Tampassuk climate is certainly more suitable for the canes. It also appeared to him that the canes grown at Tampassuk by natives, without any care, were finer than those under cultivation elsewhere. There is a rapid about a mile above the Residency, which would give water-power for the necessary works.

There are no powerful fighting tribes in any part of the Cession, as there are at Sarawak, so that there need be no difficulty or bloodshed in establishing order and security throughout the country. "The few turbulent spirits will soon subside when they find there is an armed force ready and able to avenge any lawless act they may commit." At Tampassuk, Pangeran, Sree Rajah Muda is the most influential chief, and he has gone in heartily with the Company, and renders them every assistance in his power. Mr. Dobree heard at Labuan that several shops had sprung up at Pappar, which shows that confidence has been established among the natives. Since his visit to North Borneo nearly three years of steady exploration and administrative work have fully endorsed his belief, that the Company will have no difficulty in exercising its powers and bringing about a rule of security and order.

IV.

Mr. F. Witti, in the special employ of the Company, lately as Assistant Resident at Tampassuk, and an experienced pioneer, courageous in venturing upon unknown tracks, exploring strange rivers, visiting villages where the white man has never been seen, has made excursions into the heart of the territory, and has everywhere been received with kindness, not only by the headmen of villages, but by the natives themselves. Mr. Witti, during 1880 and 1881, has transmitted to London several diaries of his official excursions. One of his earliest reports relates to a journey which he made to the oil shale at the

Sekuati River, and to an exploration overland from Marudu Bay to Pappar. Attended by guides and accompanied by a small party of coolies in the Company's employ, he left the Abai in the Residency's prahu on November 4th, 1880. He went ashore at Agar Point and walked to the mouth of the Sekuati, which occupied about an hour. The white cliffs shown on the Admiralty chart are situated at the common mouth of the Sekuati and the Kurnia Rivers. He found the banks of these rivers uninhabited. At Kurnia Creek, a cable's length from the mouth, he found oil emanating from the river-bed. In the sunlight the water was beautifully iridescent. When the tide was out on the following day he made holes where the oil was oozing out, and soon had for each small excavation a spring yielding oil and water; the surrounding soil was found highly bituminous for a surface extent of eighty square yards. To fill several jars with crude petroleum took merely the time required to raise it from the improvised well. He also filled two kerosine cases with the matrix itself. As he bored a couple of yards deep, he found that the proportion of bitumen evidently increased. The rock near the well is ordinary clay containing some hydrated oxide of iron; he cannot say on what that formation may rest, but in digging he now and then came on pieces of very massive lignite. Outside those eighty square yards no bitumen could be found, but he did not, however, carry his research far. The ebb-stream brought no indications of petroleum from up country, and people say this is the only outcrop known. The Illanuns formerly used the solidified petroleum to give the bottoms of their prahus a coating. Examples of the oil were sent to England, and have since been chemically investigated with interesting results.*

* "NOTES ON A NATURAL OIL OBTAINED FROM AN 'OIL SHALE' IN NORTH BORNEO.

"ROYAL COLLEGE OF CHEMISTRY,
"SOUTH KENSINGTON, *August 9th*, 1881.

"The substance as secured, mixed with water, is a thick oil or bitumen, with a not unpleasant odour.

"The thick oily portion was distilled in steam, that is, it was placed in a retort with water raised to 100° C., and steam from a small boiler forced in. When thus treated, a considerable quantity of oil came over with water, from which it was separated by means of a globe. When dried by calcic chloride and submitted to distillation, the greater part was found to boil at about 230°-245° C., although some oil began to come over at 200°. The portion distilling between 230°-240° was collected apart. It formed a beautiful clear oil, with a slight camphoric odour. It evaporates very slowly when exposed to the air, as might be expected from its high boiling-point. It is not affected by exposure to the atmosphere; a sample placed in a porcelain dish retained its clearness for a long period.

"It burns alone with a smoky, highly luminous flame, and with a lamp-wick gives a light of an intensity equal to the best petroleum.

V.

On the 9th of November Mr. Witti reached Layer-Layer, where the Sultan received him in full dress, and was not easily persuaded to save his gunpowder. Various other chiefs came in. Amongst these Illanuns

The mean composition of the distilled oil as determined by numerous analyses was as follows :

Carbon	82 per cent.
Hydrogen	10 ,,
Oxygen	8 ,,
	100

" It is not, however, a petroleum of the ordinary kind (which are all hydrocarbons, that is, consist of carbon and hydrogen only), but a mixture of at least two substances ; one of which is a petroleum, or paraffin oil, and the other an oxidised body which, as far as the examination of the small amount would allow of an opinion being formed, is of the nature of a terpene; in other words, closely related to the camphors. When larger quantities are operated upon, it will, no doubt, be found that the separation of these two bodies is an easy matter ; and this separation will be going on at the place of natural occurrence; the thicker part, or tarry portion, containing the oxidised constituent of the oil. . . . From the presence of this oxidised substance it would seem that the geological formation is a recent one, probably tertiary. The strata at the point of occurrence will be found inclined several degrees, and cut through by a stream at a fault in the vicinity. If a boring be made in the beds there is little doubt that a quantity of oil would be obtained and could be easily worked. In some cases oils may be used direct for burning, but when distilled this oil would be very useful either as a luminant or for lubricating purposes. The sample operated on by us had probably been exposed for some time

every adult is, if not a slave, at least a Datu. He noticed here half-a-dozen females weaving Sarong cloth. At night he put up at the "big house" of the village of Tigaman, where the natives, from being at first somewhat reserved, became very friendly. Thence he travelled by road and river to Moroli. *En route* he says: "Emerging on the Sonchum Reach, we saw two females in the midst of the swollen stream struggling against being swept away; up to their waists in the water, heavy loads on their backs, a single weak prop, and the younger Dusun girl clinging to the elder one—and the roaring rapid but a few yards off. Thus we found them making an attempt

to the air, as the percentage of light boiling oil was small. As obtained from a boring, the quantity of these light boiling bodies would, of course, be greater than where the oil has been exposed to evaporation. It will be very easy to separate these lighter oils from those containing oxygen by distillation on a large scale, when also, probably, the oxidised body may be obtained in a solid form. In this case, if it be really a camphor, its value will be much greater than an ordinary petroleum. The best kinds of native or natural pitch are formed by the slow oxidation of these already partially-oxidised carbon-hydrogen bodies, and in this case there will be an accompanying natural deposit of this substance at the points of natural oxidation, and when distilled a useful pitch will be obtained as residual matter after the lighter oils have come over. Simple filtration through sand might be sufficient to separate the oil in a state pure enough for ordinary illuminating purposes.

"FRANK HATTON, F.C.S., A.I.C.
"W. R. HODGKINSON, Ph.D."

to ford the river, but they were extricated in time.
The remarkable thing was that the poor girls in their
predicament did not scream at all, although their
becoming upset entailed drowning." At Moroli he
found the natives differed considerably in their clothing and ornaments from those they left in the morning
of the same day.

" The men wear their head-dress in form of a nightcap, and tie it
down to the lower jaw, which makes them appear as if they had
toothache. Then the men wear armlets, hip circles, earrings, and
that awkward spiral round the neck, like the girls up Kudat; their
ordinary dress, however, consists in the fig-leaf waist-cloth and
nothing else. I noticed females who wore a jacket without sleeves,
made of some fibre. Their complexion is remarkably light; but
that cannot make us sympathise with them, as they are rather a
suspicious lot. I doubt if they will assist to-morrow morning in
carrying our luggage, as the Kinoroms did, as far as this place;
being paid for it of course."

At Tolungan, made up of the villages of Sesapan
and Bundo, the natives welcomed Mr. Witti and his
companions. The men here tattoo themselves.

"The effect produced is quite the same as frequently seen on a
stripped 'Jack.' I told our self-pricked friends here that white men
do the same thing, for this and that reason—though I am not aware
really of any reason at all; however, I thus learnt that tattooing here
distinguishes the men who have slain a foe in an inter-tribal war.
There are five such warriors in the three houses of Bundo. The
ornament begins below the stomach and rises to the shoulders, like
the skirt of a coat, then down the upper arms; here the two or

three parallel broad stripes end, and the fore-arm on its inner side shows a number of narrow stripes. These latter are more numerous if the man-slayer be at the same time well-to-do."

A few days' travel and Mr. Witti halted at Mituo, where Kina Balu was seen free from its load of clouds just long enough for a bearing: 276°, or say from Mituo, W. ¾ N. The country here is much undulated—not one acre of level land; and the high range bordering the eastern slopes of Kina Balu appears still more distinct than from Moroli. In this district he met another set of natives. They proved to be agreeable and friendly, and in appearance compared favourably with the Dusuns on the west coast, being a finer set of men. "They are not more savage either, although many of them are tattooed, and all use the blowpipe (in Dusun 'sopok,' not 'sampitan'), as their main weapon. To the one end of the blowpipe is always made fast a spear-blade. They never heard the report of a rifle; and believed us that it was much better never to become acquainted with firearms in any way. I noticed the homespun of these people is not uniform bluish-gray, but striped with black."

VI.

About the 22nd of November, 1880, Mr. Witti's expedition reached Koligan. At various points *en route* there were numerous spring-traps set in the bush, which had no warning tablets about them but for the keen eye of the native Dusun. His guide pointed out how those traps are constantly set close by the footpath, which path itself is often quite obscured. Wild pigs and wild buffaloes abound in the forests, as also deer and other game; and a travelling party could always procure some food in these regions. But the larger animals, such as elephants, rhinoceros, and tapirs, are totally absent. The natives were astonished on being told that the ivory handle of a kris belonging to one of Witti's men was carved out of the tusk of an animal living in herds down the Kinabatangan. The men hereabouts wear on a rattan-string round their neck a short knife, the handle of which is invariably a boar's tusk. It is quite an effective addition to their scanty wearing apparel. Here at Koligan Mr. Witti saw the first glazed potteryware inland, or rather the Dusuns themselves offered it for barter; one piece was a sort of teapot representing a fantastic bird, the other a miniature jar. " Their parting so easily with these articles would imply that the old china craze has not penetrated to this secluded village."

At Danao he found an interesting custom prevailing, in the fashion of welcoming a visitor. The young wife of the headman met Mr. Witti as he entered the village. She moistened some rice in a small bamboo. "I had then to open my hand, and she poured some grains on it, after which the rice was again put back into the bamboo. This opened their hospitality, and I may subsequently partake of their rice and betel. They are not so barbarous as to call me 'Tuan,' they simply say 'Pinai,' which means friends."

Formerly the Danao Dusuns were head-hunters. In the house of the headman here there are still preserved three dozen skulls, forming no doubt an heirloom. Among the skulls in question, Witti noticed two which were taken from children, and it is remarkable how firmly set and how white the teeth in all of them are. Previous travellers have shown that in the head-hunting districts of Borneo, small heads, those of women and children, are considered most honourable, as evincing especial courage in the captors, it being understood that the tribes attacked would fight hard for their women and children.

Walking on from Makal towards Pinowantei, a herd of buffaloes was met, on what might be called in this

part a flat meadow. Buffaloes here are reared for no
other purpose than food. They are of a heavy breed.
The mountain slopes are not practicable for cattle,
and the people as yet know nothing of the plough.
A buffalo is here worth twenty tinokals, or forty
dollars, while at Tampassuk a fine riding bull costs
twelve dollars. The tinokal at two dollars forms the
unit of value, and is taken from a small gong-like
instrument. "Nobody remembers buffaloes being
brought from outside into this tract of very difficult
ground, else it would offer a chance for traders from
the coast." The hill rice is sometimes grown on
declivities of forty-five degrees. The necessary
recourse to that alone excludes any fitness of this
soil for higher objects of planting. The rice is of a
peculiar description, retaining a reddish colour even
after being boiled.

"These Dusuns have a way of their own in striking fire. Steel
and flint is replaced by a fragment of china and a small bamboo
cane. Their tinder is sure to burn on the first stroke. From fire to
water: pipes of bamboo are laid at the crossings of most of the
numerous streamlets, and also lead to the fields, forming neat little
fountains (native aqueduct)."

At Margis and Tambunan, where the expedition
arrived on November 29th, the women knew nothing
of foreign cotton-yarn, while their sisters "up Sugut"
know it and like it; "but these here are as keen on

needles as those." Needle in Dusun means a human
parasite of a very disagreeable kind, and the natives
here are sadly infested "with that wingless, hemip-
terous insect." "We yesterday passed a number of
rustic damsels whose hair was quite carroty from
neglect." This may have given rise to the report of
fair-haired people living somewhere to the south.

The Tambunanians appear to indulge occasionally
in a little head-hunting. There were many skulls in
one old man's house, some of which looked very fresh
indeed. The lower jawbone was wanting in them.
The taste of the Dusuns in this respect is manifold.
In most villages the skulls of monkeys are preserved;
in others those of deer or pig; in many only the lower
jaws of deer, the carapaces of land-tortoises, the
bladders of goats, and the drumsticks of fowls.
However, the collection of crania here, at first sight,
unnerved Witti's men a little, considering that the
Dusuns were pouring in while the inspection was
going on. Later in the evening the expedition managed
to get up a concert and dance; and after that all
enjoyed a quiet sleep. No white men ever visited
Tambunan before, and the people eagerly questioned
the travellers as to where they came from. In the
first part of their journey they were asked: "Where
are you going to?"

VII.

Early in December, Mr. Witti found himself at
Tungao, getting there by following the course of the
Pappar. The river meanders west, south, west,
south; in a few reaches it sweeps round as far as
S.S.E. the one, and N.W. the other way. At 900 feet
above sea-level, it is already as wide as down at the
Residency, but it is bouldered up and forms many
rapids. At a level of 1200 feet above sea a fall occurs,
the water dropping from about nine feet. The Dusuns
call that "Wasch." Where the banks are bold, the
river takes its sharp turns and causes landslips.
These require an ascent and a descent of 100 feet
each way, and the footing of a goat would answer best
for such scrambles. Thus, while moving for the
greater part in the shallow water, Witti had to make
many a "portage" without employing rafts. The
banks are in many places rocky. The river flows in a
bed of sandstone. Now and then the rock shows a
slaty structure, and in one place, just below Tungao,
the right bank is built up of conglomerate. The
fords were found to be between two and three feet
deep. The affluents to the Pappar in this part are
the Kalangan, the Purog, the Ponobukan, and the
Tikuh. Villages and hamlets succeed each other

down river: Tapa, Buntingnabai, Purog, Romit, Kapa, Ponobukan, Kobulu, Boyan, and Tungao.

Mr. Witti arrived at the Residency at Tampassuk early in December, having been away a month and two days. The rafts with his companions turned up in due course. Of the thirty-three miles which he floated down the river, the names of villages and affluents to the Pappar River are only partly recorded, but the course of the river is put down more accurately. It continues in a W.S.W. direction, until some fourteen miles from the Residency, when its windings mostly turn W.N.W. Of the last four miles only a single reach lies W.S.W.; all the others between W.N.W. and N.N.W. The line from Pappar village to the Residency Pappar lies W. by S. Beginning from Kagaban village, both banks present one continuous cocoa-nut plantation, interspersed with numerous hamlets and single houses.

The whole course of the Pappar River, as traced by Mr. Witti, may be computed at fifty-five miles—that is, between Pappar village and the Company's station. Its navigability ceases some twelve miles above the latter place, say sixteen miles from the river mouth. The last dangerous rapid is about twenty miles distant. The river meanders a good deal; none of the reaches are longer than half a mile, and most of them are only two cable-lengths. The Pappar could by no means be called an outlet for the rich district of Tambunan. A sort of outlet exists at the Patatan, but only for valuable produce, as gutta and beeswax. Whether anything reaches the coast by way of the Nabai country and the Kimanis Mr. Witti does not know. The experienced Abang Drahman, Resident Everett's right-hand man, told him that the Tambunan people go by the name of the "Great Dayaks," that they are rather avoided by traders, and never associated with by other adjacent tribes.

VIII.

During this and other excursions Mr. Witti, and Mr. W. B. Pryer, the Company's Resident at Sandakan, have exploded some of the most cherished fictions of geographical history, more particularly that of the wonderful lake of Kina Balu. In a paper read before the Royal Geographical Society, February 4th, 1881, Mr. William M. Crocker said :

"There are several lakes in Borneo; the largest is supposed to be Lake Kina Balu, which in all existing maps of Borneo is marked as lying to the southward of the Kina Balu Mountain, in the newly-acquired territory of the North Borneo Company. Mr. J. Hunt, who communicated an account of Borneo, in 1812, to Sir Stamford Raffles, reported the existence of this lake. Mr. Spenser St. John, who ascended Kina Balu, and who had a good view over the country lying to the south and south-east, says that it certainly does not lie in that direction, where he says there is a large plain. But a man who accompanied Mr. St. John said that he had traded with the villages on the banks of the lake, and asserted that, standing on the beach, he could not see the other side.

"Mr. St. John must have lived long enough in Borneo to know the value of native reports. Not long since I passed the night in a Dayak house in the Sadong district, where I met an old man who informed me that he was a Malow—one of a tribe living on the upper waters of the Kapuas. He assured me in the most solemn manner that he had seen men with tails. He said he ascended the Kapuas to near its source, and then walked across to the head of the Banjer, which rises near a very high mountain named 'Batu Bulan' (moonstone). Here he fell in with a tribe of men with tails. He could not speak their language, but he and his friend managed to make themselves understood, and were treated very kindly by them. They remained seven days and nights amongst the tribe. Both men and women had tails.* They wore bark of trees as a covering, through which a hole was made for the tail to pass through; they planted paddy, and lived in long houses. These and other particulars he recounted, which gave a colouring of truth to his statements. I have heard

---

* Mr. Carl Bock, in his interesting narrative of travel up the Mahakkam and down the Barito, published under the title of "The Head-Hunters of Borneo," heard of people with tails at the village of Dassa, a settlement of the Beona Dayaks. Carl Bock wonders if "Mr. Darwin received the first suggestion of his theory of man's simian descent from the fables concerning the existence of tailed men which obtained credence among so many uncivilised people." Such definite statements were made to the traveller in this village that he ultimately, with the consent of the ruling authority, sent one Tjiropon, who had seen the tailed people in an adjacent country, on an expedition to bring two of them safely to Dutch territory. The messenger was well paid, and credited with letters from his chief to the Sultan of Passir, in whose territories the tailed people were said to exist. Some time afterwards Carl Bock returned to Passir. Tjiropon gave a meagre account of his mission. He had seen the

these stories continually from other sources, but I am convinced these wonders are all invented by Dayaks and travellers, who have returned from long journeys into the interior, for the purpose of magnifying their own importance.

"From personal experience of lakes in Borneo, I am inclined to think that the numerous rivers which no doubt descend the Kina Balu mountain in the rainy season would naturally overflow the plain mentioned by Mr. St. John as lying to the southward, and that the district thus inundated, having been visited by native travellers, has been mistaken for a lake."

Since this paper was read and discussed Mr. Crocker's theory has been fully confirmed, more particularly by Mr. Pryer and Mr. Witti, who, in their explorations of the country south of Kina Balu mountain found no lake in or near the position marked on the maps.

Sultan of Passir, and had delivered to him the letter of his Highness of Koetei, but he had seen no tailed people this time, though "before Allah" he swore he had long ago. With great difficulty Mr. Bock organised another party of inquiry, with the following result :

"After twenty-five days' absence the party returned with an interesting communication from the Sultan of Passir. It appeared that Tjiropon had after all delivered the letter from the Sultan of Koetei, in which the latter potentate asked his royal cousin to send him two of the *Orang boentoet*, or 'tail people;' but the letter had been misunderstood by the Sultan of Passir. The suite in attendance upon him were known collectively as the *Orang boentoet di Sultan di Passir*—literally the 'tail people of the Sultan of Passir;' and his Highness, taking offence at the supposed request of his brother ruler that two of his personal attendants—in fact, his confidential men— should be sent to him, had waxed exceedingly wroth, and, calling Tjiropon before him, he ordered him to depart immediately. 'If the Sultan of Koetei wants my *Orang boentoet*,' said he, 'let him fetch them himself.' And so the Sultan of Passir, expecting an attack

There were some other points brought forward at
the meeting of the Royal Geographical Association in
question which it will not be out of place to allude to
here. Mr. Crocker, for instance, referring to the map
of the Indian Archipelago, demonstrated how desirable
it is to England that, with our present possessions
in the Straits of Malacca and China, and the importance of our commercial relations in the far
East, we should still further strengthen our position in those seas, the opportunity for which is
afforded by North and North-west Borneo. "The
splendid harbours on these coasts, in which the
combined fleets of the world could ride in safety, and
the unlimited supply of coal, secure a commanding

---

from the Sultan of Koetei in response to his challenge, had been
arming himself ever since, erecting fortifications, and preparing for
war. The letter from Mr. Meijer had satisfactorily explained matters,
and put his Highness at his ease. His mistake was, perhaps, par-
donable, for he sent word that the only *Orang boentoet* he had ever
heard of were those, so called, forming his suite."

It seems to me that the author of "The Head-Hunters of
Borneo" unconsciously offers in his illustrations a possible explanation of the current fiction. His Bornean hunter wears an outer
skin in such a way that the tail of it might in the distance be
mistaken for a human dorsal appendage; while the scant toilette
of the Dayak boys lends itself to the same idea. Natives of tribes
not cultivating this kind of dress might naturally enough speak of
others as *Orang boentoet*, and native travellers desiring to exalt
their own importance may have invented the living tail out of the
ornamental one.

position in the event of a naval war. Already the
Russians possess strongly-fortified settlements on the
Manchurian coast to the north of China, and are said
to covet the commodious havens of the Korea, where
their daily increasing fleets might find protection. It is
therefore manifestly of paramount importance to British
interests and trade that England should maintain her
supremacy in those waters by securing those advantages
in Borneo which are now within her grasp, and which
can be acquired with such evident benefit to the nation."
Lord Aberdare, the President of the Geographical Society, in introducing Mr. Crocker, said that gentleman
had peculiar advantages for obtaining a knowledge
of his subject, "inasmuch as he had spent no less than
sixteen years of his life at Sarawak, and had taken an
active interest in all its affairs. During a large part of
the time he had officiated as Resident, and during the
absence of Rajah Brooke he had administered the
affairs as President of the Administrative Committee.
Throughout the whole period he had taken an intelligent interest in the interior of Borneo, an island
second only in size to Australia, and which contained,
probably, nearly as much unknown land as any other
portion of the globe of equal dimensions."

Lord Aberdare also made some observations at
the close of the meeting, bearing upon a question
referred to several times in the course of this work,

and somewhat eloquently exploited in the graphic details of a river-trip described by the Resident at Sandakan in the chapter following this. I mention these succeeding pages here, feeling that the general reader may find the present chapter, possibly, over-weighted with the political and economic aspects of the new cession to British enterprise and money. Lord Aberdare, in proposing a vote of thanks to Mr. Crocker, is reported, in the "Proceedings of the Royal Geographical Society," to have said :

"Englishmen are very apt to consider themselves the great colonisers of the world, and indeed they have done a work of which they may justly be proud. They have taken possession of and extended themselves over immense tracts of country, which are likely to perpetuate a race as vigorous and enterprising as our own; but there are certain climatic conditions which oppose their spreading in every region of the world. Although men like Sir James Brooke and Mr. Alfred Dent may lead the way in civilising districts at present inhabited by barbarous or semi-barbarous people, it is quite clear that Borneo can never be settled altogether by persons of English race; and as it seems to be the fate of inferior races to give way to others more energetic, it is probable that the huge islands of the Eastern Seas will in process of time be inhabited by descendants of the Chinese race. There is, however, one great feature of present times which cannot be overlooked. Unfortunately, it cannot be said that wars have ceased, but they are now generally on a comparatively small scale, and the devastation caused by them is slight indeed when contrasted with that of the wars of past days. I believe that if an accurate census could have been taken in India at the time that England became possessed of it, and if another were taken at the present day, it would be found that the population has increased by upwards of 50,000,000. No doubt, as Asia becomes more and more under the domination of the three great empires, Russia, China, and Great Britain, the population will increase enormously, and in process of time overflow to the south, just as in ancient times it overflowed to the west. The west is now too strongly occupied to permit of wholesale immigration. In all probability China, with its 400,000,000 inhabitants, is destined to find an outlet in the magnificent islands to the south. The Chinese constitution is fitted to the climate which persons of the English race are unable to stand."

IX.

The subject of the influence of England and other naval powers in the Eastern Seas, and more particularly in the Pacific, was carefully considered by an essayist in "The Edinburgh Review" of July, 1880, the occasion being a critical review of Ravensteiu's "Russians on the Amoor," Bax's "Eastern Seas," Colomb's "Russian Development and our Naval and Military Positions in the North Pacific," and Paul Gaffarel's "Les Colonies Françaises." It was here shown that the English population of our colonial possessions in the year of the Great Exhibition of 1851, was not more than two millions, reckoning them up in all parts of the world ; while to-day the colonies in the South Pacific alone contain nearly three millions of inhabitants of European descent. Their united revenues are greater than that of many an ancient and important state in Europe. The total value of their imports and exports is nearly a hundred millions sterling. The statistics of their realised wealth, of their railways, their telegraphs, their post-offices, and their shipping, compare favourably with those of many far-earlier-settled communities. Important as they are, however, and closely as they are connected with the mother country by the ties of commerce as well as of nationality and loyal affection, our inter-course with them includes but a part, and not the greater part, of our commercial interests in the Pacific Ocean. The exchange of commodities—exclusive of bullion—between the United Kingdom and our great dependencies at the Antipodes reaches in money value a total of about forty millions of pounds sterling. With our other possessions and the foreign countries which may be taken as belonging to the "Pacific system," we have a trade reaching a value of nearly sixty millions. In fact, about one-sixth of the whole external commerce of Great Britain is carried on with the states and colonies which compose it.

Hydrographically and strategically considered this colonial system may be said to extend from the Straits of Malacca on the west to the American coast on the east, and from Russian Tartary on the Amoor, to Southern Chili and Tasmania. It comprises the whole seaboard of the Chinese Empire and of Western America, north and south, besides the great Dutch, French, and Spanish colonies. Our business relations

I

with these countries are intimate and extensive. With the treaty ports of China and with Hong Kong we exchange annually upwards of twenty million pounds' worth of goods. With Japan we do a business of over three millions, with the Philippines of more than two, and with the Dutch islands three and a half. With French Cochin-China, Siam, and our Straits Settlements our yearly trade amounts to close on five. On the other side of the ocean the figures of our commerce with the Spanish American Republics amount to about twelve millions; whilst a still larger sum would represent the value of our increasing intercourse with California and of our transactions with the remaining countries.

In addition to these figures the British carrying trade is mentioned. In the year 1877, exclusive of the coasting trade, the tonnage of ships entered and cleared in the Australasian ports was 6,394,529 British, and 608,963, or less than one-tenth, foreign. About four-fifths of the transport of commodities to and from the Chinese Empire by sea are effected in vessels carrying the British flag. Lines of steamers flying the same ensign pass and repass across the South pacific from Panama to the Antipodes, along the coast of South America, and between Japan and China and our possessions in Australia and Malacca.

Even these impressive facts take no account of the

enormous trade between our colonies throughout the
world and the several Pacific States on both sides of
the ocean, and the food that comes for our home
population from the Port of San Francisco.

The Pacific Ocean occupies nearly one half of the
whole surface of the globe. Its extent is greater than
that of all the dry land. Other Powers beside our
own possess important dependencies in its western
portion, near our own colonies and our great trade
routes. Between the Straits Settlements and Hong
Kong lies the French colony of Cochin-China. Not
far from the coast of Queensland are the islands of
the New Caledonian group, which have been
in the hands of the French for nearly thirty years.
Fiji lies between them and the cluster of islands in
the South Pacific, Taïti, Tuamotu, and the Marquesas,
which last are also dependencies of France. The
Dutch Indies of the Archipelago are neighbours of
our settlements in the Straits of Malacca and at
Labuan. Portugal still retains a memory of her
former conquests in the island of Timor. The great
group of the Spanish Philippines lines one of the old
routes to the Chinese ports. On the other side British
Columbia marches with the territory of the United
States, both on the north and on the south. Colonial
possessions of all the maritime powers, with the
exception of the British province just named, lie

only in the western and southern portions of the Pacific. Along the whole eastern side, from Vancouver to the Straits of Magellan, there is a wide belt of water, in which islands rarely occur. This circumstance tends to complicate considerably the question of providing coaling stations for the steam fleets which already traverse its great spaces, and for the squadrons to which some day or other the rapidly-increasing commerce may have to look for protection.

"One of the most powerful of European nations has for many years had a footing on the shores of the Pacific; though, having first made her way to them by land, her possessions are continental rather than insular. Russia is the owner of great tracts of coast on the North Pacific; and though of late years she has resigned her American territory to the United States, with the adjoining group of the Aleutian islands, she has compensated herself by extending the southern limit of her Amoor province of Eastern Siberia to the frontier of Corea; whilst her cession of the Kuriles to Japan has given her undivided ownership of Sakhalin, which is close to, and forms but an outwork of, her possessions on *terra firma*. The development of the Russian Empire in this quarter has not been watched in this country with the interest which it deserves. The history of her colonisation of the remote regions drained by the Amoor and its tributaries and washed by the waters of the Seas of Tartary and Okhotsk is a record of adventure, persistence, and conquest of hardships, which is well worth attention."

The essayist, after an exhaustive examination of the strength of the Russian naval position in the Pacific as compared with our own and every other power, dwells upon the great desirability of England's

possessing an island station in the waters between
Japan and Corea, or off the southern extremity
of the latter peninsula. In the absence of such a
possession it would seem that the only course open
to a navy called upon to protect the trade of
this country against cruisers issuing from the
Siberian ports would be to attack and destroy the
ships which they might contain. One significant
anecdote may be given, which will explain with much
distinctness what the escape of a cruising squadron
from those harbours would imply as against our
commercial interests in the Pacific. When, towards
the end of 1878, the late Prime Minister was presented with a gold box by the British residents in
San Francisco, the spokesman of the deputation,
Mr. Harrison, said in the course of his address : " We
had thirteen Russian cruisers lying in our harbour, and
some 600,000 or 700,000 tons of shipping about
leaving it."* As the greater part of the cargoes of
the ships whose sailing depended upon the event of
peace or war, was composed of food for this country,
we may concede that there was something more than
mere business interests that might have had to look
to our navy for protection.

* Commander Gurdon, R.N., says ("Journal of Royal United
Service Institution," vol. xxi. p. 686) : "I have seen 70,000 tons
of British shipping lying at anchor at one time in the harbour
of San Francisco."

The Russian naval force in the Pacific has been recently increased. There are 15,000 troops maintained in the Amoor region, most of them in or near the coast ports. Several battalions of riflemen are formed out of the local settlers. Some of these extensions were made in view of possible troubles with China. We have a respectable force in these distant waters; but in the north-western portion of the Pacific we have no coaling stations north of Hong Kong which would be available in war. Japan and China would supply us with coal, but they belong to the family of nations, and would be entitled to issue proclamations of neutrality, and they have fleets which are not to be despised as engines for compelling a proper international observance thereof. The Russian ships would have the enormous advantage of a long line of coast and many harbours to which they could resort, where they would find plenty of fuel and supplies of all kinds procured on the spot or brought to them by a land route quite secure against attacks from hostile ships. No other European power has the same resources on the spot.

X.

The cutting of the Panama Canal will sooner or later attract increased attention to our interests in the Pacific. Trade may be attracted into fresh routes and demand new means of protection. Touching the North Pacific, General Selby Smyth, commanding the military forces of Canada, in a report published last year, speaks of the inadequate force at Victoria, and directs attention to the fact that Vancouver is only 4500 miles from Petrapaulovsk, and that the Amoor is barely 500 miles farther off.

"'In the event of war,' he says, 'Russia would be in a position to harass not only Hong Kong and the China and Japan trade, but to send a squadron across the ocean in thirty days to attack the western seaport of the Dominion. Our security in the Pacific requires Esquimalt to be well guarded; our fleets must keep the sea, if necessary, in all weathers, and they cannot do so without coal. That important element is in ample stock and of prime quality at Nanaimo. The British navy is scattered over the Pacific, and there were no works of defence at Vancouver till last year ; no forts for the protection of our coal ; nothing but British prestige and a few companies of militia at Victoria and up the Fraser River.'"

Upon this, and other points of equal importance, the Edinburgh Reviewer comes to the conclusion

that few will care to deny that our whole naval
position in the Pacific Ocean has undergone an important change ; and without for a moment regarding
other powers jealously, with every wish to be respectful to Russia, and only desirous of maintaining our
own, it would be a grave mistake should we shut our
eyes to the changing necessities of our maritime forces
in the Eastern Seas. "Interests, which thirty years
ago we could hardly have considered very important,
have attained dimensions which render their protection a matter worthy of serious consideration. A
great colonial empire has grown up there in the
interval, which not only promises to increase in
wealth and size, but which also draws to it more and
more of our trade, and is now holding out the hope
of aiding in the supply of food which we require. A
large proportion of the capital of the country invested
in shipping and the cargoes carried by it is con-
tinuously employed in the commerce of the Pacific.
Throughout its wide spaces we have but few resting-
places for our ships. We have no real basis for naval
operations between Sydney, Vancouver, and Hong
Kong. The days in which the coast ports of Spanish
America monopolised nearly the whole of the tonnage
sailing on its waters under our flag have quite gone by.
New routes upon it are every day being followed.
At the same time powers far more formidable than

the turbulent republics of the South and Central American coast, or than the Celestial Empire, have gained a footing on its shores. If ever our navy should be called upon to protect our trade against an enemy, it will not be in the Pacific that the least important portion of its duties will be performed."

The geographical and strategical position of British North Borneo formed a leading topic at a meeting held at the Westminster Palace Hotel, March 26th, 1879, to discuss the affairs of the new cession. Mr. Thomas Sutherland, chairman of the Peninsular and Oriental Steamship Company, in speaking of the important geographical position of North Borneo, said: "It is an exceedingly advantageous position from a political point of view for England to control. The great majority of those who are here, I presume, like myself, have some particular acquaintance with the East, more particularly with the China Sea, therefore it must appear to them with far greater force now than ever, that in our commerce we are at a great loss for the want of a sufficient and commodious harbour between the two places to which we now trade, namely, Singapore and Hong Kong. If we can only gain the advantage of having a port so conveniently situated and so admirably suited for strategical purposes, and if we can gain the great advantage of prosecuting there an entirely new trade which this country of ours requires so much at the present moment, I think I need say no more in favour of the resolution which I now submit to the meeting : 'That North Borneo holds such a position geographically in the midst of the China Sea, midway between the great trading centres of Singapore and Hong Kong, with exceptionally good harbours and coal supplies, as will at no distant date render its occupation of undoubted importance to the commerce and interests of this country as a great maritime power.' "

Admiral Keppel, addressing himself to another branch of the same subject, said :

"I think I can state from personal experience that there is no place in the Eastern Seas so well adapted, so far as the coast and harbours are concerned, as this is, and so well calculated to protect the trade or any establishment which may be formed there. The first thing I can naturally suppose for any Government to consider would be likely to be this: Whether or not protection can be afforded to those who expend their capital in this proposed settlement? Now, I can find no place so easily defended as this place could be, at so little expense to the Government. With one or two gunboats at the outside (natives have a very great respect for that small class of vessel), together with the assistance of the torpedo, of which we have lately heard so much, I think the whole coast could be very easily defended. There is the harbour of Gaya, which is one of the finest harbours in the world and capable of holding any amount of shipping, and there is a larger harbour on the eastern coast called Sandakan. That would be of the same importance on the east coast as the harbour of Gaya on the western coast, the latter, however, being more in the line of the traffic between China and Singapore and other ports."

Referring to the political aspect of the cession, which Sir Douglas Forsyth had mentioned in a speech approving of the desirability of the Government supporting the efforts of the association, Sir Rutherford Alcock said :

"Then there is the political point of view which Sir Douglas Forsyth touched upon very successfully and properly. No doubt every proposal to occupy any new land—whatever its advantages may be—will meet with some amount of opposition from the common argument, that it does not matter whether you make it a colony or only allow British subjects to go there; they will sooner or later got into a quarrel, and will want protection, and then we shall have the cost and the trouble and anxiety of protecting them. I think in my introductory observations I almost met that objection by anticipation. It is impossible to conceive, in the present state of the world, that such a tempting territory as Borneo, with one if not two of the finest harbours in the Eastern Seas, will long remain unoccupied by other Powers. It becomes a question, then, whether it should be occupied under the British flag, or by those who may be our enemies. Now, looking to our possessions in this part of the world, and to the fact that this is right in the fair way to them, certainly if this territory were in the hands either of Russia or of any other of the European powers with whom we might unfortunately be at war, it would make a very material difference in any efforts we might make to carry on our commerce without molestation. Gaya as a port not only might be very easily defended by any Power in possession, but it would afford protection to privateers and ships of war which might dash out on this line of commerce; and even a large fleet like ours would hardly be able to protect it. If it were, on the contrary, in our possession, we should have shelter for our own ships instead of having others thus sheltered to attack us, and from whence we could look out for any privateers or fleet which might attempt to disturb the even course of our commerce."

XI.

It would seem, then, that the chief hope of civilising and making prosperous the islands of the Indian Archipelago lies in the power to attract the very class of labour which America has obtained from China, with power to control and economise it. At the meeting just mentioned, Mr. Errington, M.P., who takes a deep and active interest in the welfare of all natives, spoke with satisfaction of the fact that the new Company would only employ free labour. "The meeting," he said, "will be glad to observe the great advantages which Borneo possesses in this respect from its position, being within such easy reach of the Chinese coast, from which ample supplies of free labour may be obtained. In other places, not so circumstanced, it is necessary to have recourse to the system of indentured coolie labour. I believe it is admitted that Chinese labour needs no such indenture system. Therefore, by the mere encouragement of free immigration from China, you will be able to supply your settlement in Borneo with ample labour, under conditions which will commend themselves to the approval of the people of this country." The vast islands of the Eastern Seas are evidently destined to become actively subject to foreign governments—the administrative power and capital being European, the labour largely Chinese.* The Dutch at Java, the English at Sarawak, have shown what can be done in this direction; and a further and probably more rapid development may be looked for in the territory of British North Borneo.

* "But the phases of character in which the Chinese possess the most interest for us Western peoples are those which so peculiarly fit them for competing in the great labour-market of the world. They are good agriculturists, mechanics, labourers, and sailors; and they possess all the intelligence, delicacy of touch, and unwearying patience which are necessary to render them first-rate machinists and manufacturers. They are, moreover, docile, sober, thrifty, industrious, self-denying, enduring, and peace-loving to a degree. They are equal to any climate, be it hot or frigid; all that is needed is teaching and guiding, combined with capital and enterprise, to convert them into the most efficient workmen to be found on the face of the earth. In support of these assertions it is only necessary to refer to our experience of them in America, Australia, India, and the Eastern Archipelago. Wherever the tide of Chinese emigration has set in, there they have proved themselves veritable working bees, and made good their footing, to the exclusion of less quiet, less exacting, less active, or less intelligent artisans and labourers. Even in China they have already proved their worth by helping to construct, under foreign superintendence, men-of-war of first-class workmanship and formidable proportions; and their artificers are daily acquiring increased skill in the arsenals now in active work at Tientsin, Shanghae, and Foochow. The marvellous energy of which they are capable as mere labourers is moreover constantly exhibited

at the port of Shanghae, where they have been known to accomplish the discharge of a ship in less time, as I have been assured, than can be effected by dock-labourers at home, even with all the appliances of cranes and otherwise which these latter have at disposal."—" *The Foreigner in Far Cathay," by Sir Walter Medhurst, formerly H.B.M. s Consul at Shanghae.*

A TRIP ON THE KINABATANGAN.

Art and Travel—The Unknown—Tropical Scenery—A hundred and
fifty miles of River never previously visited by Europeans—
Edible Birdsnest Farmers—Savagery—Tales of Blood and
Plunder—English Influences—Floating Houses—Native Men
and Women at Home—Open-air Bivouacs—Living Wonders of
the Tropics—Gorgeous Birds and Butterflies—Human Heads in
Wrong Places—At Imbok—Natives in Splendid Attire—Wild
Animals—Opportunities for Sport—The Kinabatangan of the
Future—The Vanished Race and the Coming Labourer.

I.

ART loves the shadows of gray old towers, or their
reflected images in shallow waters, rather than the
wild torrents of forest-wastes and mountains.

The English painter seeking space on the walls
of the English Academy, finds his most popular subjects in familiar stories, in domestic incident, in the
illustration of history or the current life of the times,
keeping upon the ordinary human track of existence.
If he is a landscape artist he rarely gets away from

the calm restful scenes of his own country, unless
it is to wander in the sunny lands of an ancient
civilisation.

One would have thought that the representative
painters of a great empire, which counts its chief
possessions in the tropics, would have striven to bring
home to us through the medium of their glowing
canvases a continual sense of the strange beauties of
those countries of everlasting summer. I suspect
only a great master would dare to exhibit anything
like true transcripts of Nature as she is seen at the
equator; but the etcher, the worker in black and
white, need fear no adverse criticism which the
colourist would be sure to encounter the closer he
adhered to the truth.

By an odd coincidence the other day, I had
laid down this manuscript diary of a journey along
one of the most important waterways of Sabah
near a copy of Mr. Hammerton's familiar contri-
bution to art and letters, "The Unknown River."
Everybody knows the delightful etchings with which
the author has studded his poetic pages. "The
explorer of a nameless European river," he says,
"need not hope to be remembered like Livingstone
or Speke, but he may set forth in the full assurance
of finding much that is worth finding and of enjoying
many of the sensations, deducting those connected

with personal vanity, which give interest to more famous explorations." Mr. Hammerton, of course, only speaks of his river from an art point of view. Old enough in the recorded history of the district, it had, however, not been "illustrated." He registers a qualification in this respect when he says: "It is necessary to the complete enjoyment of an excursion of discovery that the region to be explored, whether mountain or river, or whatever else it may be, should not have been explored by others, or, at any rate, not with the same objects and intentions. A geologist has a certain satisfaction in marching, hammer in hand, over a tract of country not yet conquered for geology; and an artist likes to sketch in secluded valleys where it is not probable that any artist has been before." If Mr. Hammerton or some kindred genius could only be induced to follow this liking to its extremity, and explore with pencil and etching-plate a Bornean river, the result would be some rare artistic compositions of marked and positive form, with studies of lights and shadows that would be both interesting and instructive when compared with pictorial illustrations of our northern clime. The *real* "unknown river" of Kinabatangan for example, what a companion volume it would make to Mr. Hammerton's idealised stream that hurries by the towers of Autun!

K

II.

The following notes are from the diary of an excursion up the Kinabatangan River, by Mr. Pryer, the Company's Resident at Sandakan, who explored it a distance of one hundred and fifty miles farther than it had been visited by any other European. He left Sandakan "on the 23rd February, 1881, in the steam-launch 'Boyah' (Crocodile). Mr. W. in charge of engines, an engine-driver, stoker, and steersman; my boy (a heathen Chinee) Banjer, a Banjermassin man who had been captured near that place by Balignini pirates, sold in Sooloo, and subsequently freed by me; a Sooloo pilot, in general charge of the expedition, and therefore termed 'the Commodore;' and three other Sooloos in a gobang (canoe) towing astern."

Having with some difficulty pushed through the Langan langan Manook ("in some maps another way is marked from Sandakan Bay to the Kinabatangan River, which does not exist"), they entered the lagoon district, a swamp of some forty or fifty miles in length and about twenty deep, fringed with mangroves and nepas; covered at high water, but black slime and mud at low; intersected everywhere by lagoons and backwaters.

"One of my boats was once lost here for five days, the men being reduced to great straits for want of water, and I myself, with good guides, have twice been lost for a day each time. One lagoon or creek is exactly like another, and sometimes after proceeding along one in search of the true way, we would find that we had wasted a couple of hours or more exploring a blind alley. At the back of this dreary region, its mouth debouching into, and being lost amongst the numerous lagoons, is one fine river, the Alfred, and as in the course of the day we passed no less than five large openings down which water, partly fresh, was discharged, I expect it is not the only one. In times long past the Booloodoopy tribe had its headquarters somewhere amongst these waters, choosing this strange locality so as not to be easily found by the fierce pirates constantly haunting the coast. Once, with an old Booloodoopy, one of the fathers of the tribe, as guide, I found my way through the swamps into the Alfred River, and ascended it for several miles. At the farthest point reached, it was nearly two hundred yards wide; eleven fathoms deep; fresh water; virgin forest on either bank; a rich soil; and a flat ground alternating with low hills."

Steaming up the river till ten o'clock and there anchoring for the night, Mr. Pryer's expedition went on the next morning at five, and arrived at Malape, the first sign of human dwellings seen in the river from its entrance. The village had its origin in the Gormanton caves, some 25,000 dollars' worth of birdsnests is yearly bought, and it is also at present used as the depôt for up-country produce. It is fairly prosperous, and as a mild but firm government is being introduced instead of the old Sooloo style, many people are flocking to the place, which is rapidly expanding. Starting off again about eleven o'clock, for one hour or more the expedition steamed past campongs, houses and gardens, until all signs of cultivation ceased; for seven hours afterwards nothing was seen but low thick forest on either bank.

February 24th saw the launch under way again; and all day the expedition passed through "nothing but interminable forest, without any indication of human life." Even the birds and butterflies and other tropical wonders of "wing and feather" were absent. The river rolled on in solitary state, fringed with untrodden woods. "At Seebongan," says Mr. Pryer, "I made inquiries about the prospects of sport. 'Any elephants?' '*Mataod*' (lots). 'Rhinoceros?' '*Mataod*.' 'Deer?' '*Mataod*.' 'Pigs?' '*Mataod*.' 'Buffaloes?' '*Oh! mataod sekali.*' Then a noise, something between a squeal and a snort, was heard, apparently within a few yards of the chief's house, which was dimly visible against the clear black sky: 'That's one!'"

Two days were spent here in visiting the chief and taking in wood to replace the exhausted coal. On the 27th they steamed away again, passing many abandoned clearings, about which, Banjer, an old river man, spun many yarns. Here was one chief's place, there another's; at this point Dato So-and-so fought Pangeran Someone else; in a house over there had been big "bichara" between two chiefs; here the Sultan had a "Bintang-marrow"* station (a custom-

* A Bintang-marrow station is made by slinging a rattan across the stream, for raising which a heavy duty is charged.

house); down this long reach, for miles together, the
Tunbumohas had houses and gardens on either bank,
and so forth and so on. Banjer was a Sultan's man,
and had once been put on a "Bintang-marrow"
station. The man in charge of it thought the time
had come to take a little duty in blood, just to let
people see that the Sultan didn't keep "Bintang-
marrow" stations for nothing. So they caught a
trader, accused him of evading the payment of duties,
and tying a rope round his wrists, fastened him to a
post with his feet off the ground, and left him hanging
there. He cried continually all day long: "I have
committed no fault, I have committed no fault."
They returned in the evening with their krises and
hewed him to bits. Banjer went on to tell Mr.
Pryer that he was present when the Tunbumohas
"semungup-ed" a man who was a bought slave.
The Tunbumohas tied him up with his arms out-
stretched (crucified in fact), and they danced round
him. At last the headman approached, and wishing
him a pleasant journey to Kina Balu, stuck his spear
about an inch deep, and no more, in the man's body;
and another then said, "Bear my kind remembrances
to my brother at Kina Balu," and did the same; and
in this way, with messages to deceased relatives at
Kina Balu, all those present slightly wounded the
man. When the dance was over they unbound

him, but he was dead.   This custom is known as
"semungup," and is practised by the far inland
tribes to this day. The Tunbumohas, however, having
an intuitive idea that white men might not view such
a custom with approval, have abandoned it so far that
they substitute a pig for a man.

Banjer was full of local stories of blood and
plunder. Mr. Pryer speaks of the chief (whom
Banjer calls Dato) as "Dato Haroun al Raschid,"
which gives a spice of suggested fiction to all Banjer's
stories; but, judging from the works of other recent
travellers in Borneo, they are no doubt only too true.

"Dato Haroun al Raschid once sent Banjer on an expedition to
'rampass' (plunder) a Chinese trader at Lingcabo. Taha was their
leader; there were four of them, Hasah was one (the disgraced
Commodore). Hasah was very active in picking out the Chinaman's
most valuable goods (Hasah, simpering, denies the soft impeachment,
and intimates that Banjer's alacrity on the occasion in question excited
his highest admiration). But there was one man who didn't care for
the Dato, Toongal of Pulo Guya; he came with his boats and blockaded
the Kinabatangan, and Dato Haroun sent two big boats out to fight
him, and he captured one and killed every soul on board. The other
boat escaped, but with three men of the crew killed. Then Dato
Haroun went down to Pulo Guya and smashed Toongal's jaw. What
with this on the one hand, and conferring a title on him on the
other, he prevailed upon Toongal to keep quiet for a bit. He,
however, broke out again afterwards, raided up the coast of Borneo,
and round Sooloo itself, and away up the Palawan. He never gave
any quarter, but killed everyone. When Banjer was down there the
other day in a British man-of-war, the Pulo Guya people said: 'Ah!
it's well for you you are on board a man-of-war. If it were not for

these " Engrees," with their steam-launches and breech-loading rifles,
we would kill every Soolooman we could lay our hands on, as we
used to do in the good old times.' "

Mr. Pryer finds food for pleasant reflection in the
fact that the bare knowledge that an Englishman is in
the country has stopped murders and human sacrifices,
and has confined fierce head-hunting tribes within
their own boundaries; has put an end to " Bintang
marrow " and its accompanying horrors; has caused
the fierce islanders, in a great measure, to abandon
piracy, and has put a stop to an incalculable amount
of misery, "*though plenty yet remains to be done.*"

III.

After steaming away till late in the afternoon,
at last they came to houses — two small villages,
Terbilliong and Blut, inhabited by Tunbumohas.
Amongst other people they met here the identical
Taha alluded to by Banjer, and were warmly welcomed
by him. Taha was on a trading expedition, and
occupied what is termed a "lanteen," a dwelling
which demands a word of description. It is a house,
in fact, built on a bamboo raft; Taha's raft was about
thirty feet long by twenty-four broad. About six
feet of one end was open, forming a sort of verandah,

where cooking, etc. was done. The rest had an attap
roof over it, shed fashion, about a third only being
surrounded by side walls, forming the sleeping apart-
ment, raised about three feet above the floor. In
front was a porch, giving quite an air of finish to
the whole. In this lanteen Taha could float down
comfortably, from village to village, collecting his
debts and storing his payments, which are generally
rattans, always carrying his wife and family with
him. The voyage up, with the trade goods, is done in
a canoe, the goods being sold on credit from house to
house, and the debts collected on the downward
journey.

Having visited the chief of the village, who
received him with hearty demonstrations of welcome,
the launch was tied alongside Taha's lanteen for
the night, and the next morning (February 28th),
shortly before daybreak, the expedition plunged once
more into the seemingly endless forest. Meeting at
length with difficult shallows, Mr. Pryer returned to
Blut, where he transferred a few stores to the
lanteen, kept the four Sooloos and Banjer with
him, and sent the launch back to Elopura. On
March 1st, with Banjer, the boy, four Sooloos, and
two Tunbumohas, borrowed from the village, he
started in the canoe to explore the higher part of the
river. From six in the morning till about eight in

the evening they held their way, with but three stops
of about half an hour each. As they were able to
keep alongside the bank, out of the force of the
stream, and in fact generally found a backwater that
they were able to take advantage of, they did not
travel less than forty miles. Mr. Pryer occasionally
walked alongside the boat on firm dry mud, and found
that, even in the long reaches, they managed three-
and-a-quarter to three-and-a-half miles an hour. In
fact, he was delighted at the change from the heat,
clatter, dirt, and smoke of the launch.

"The principal matter of interest seen this day was a Dayak 'long
house,' which we came on rather to my surprise. They were of the
Tungara tribe, and in their ways, manners, and customs seemed much
the same as the well-known Dayaks of Sarawak. The entrance to
the house was up a high notched post. Inside was a row of rooms on
the left hand, with doors opening into the central passage, opposite
to which, on the right, was a slightly raised platform, running the
length of the house; the whole being under one roof, and raised on
piles several feet from the ground. No one was visible on my first
entering, but the door nearest to me being ajar, I pushed it, and
going in found myself in a queer dirty little place, divided into two
or three compartments. There were two or three women and one
old man. The women crouched away, clinging together, half trying
to hide themselves, while the old man puffed away at a pipe, and
pretended not to see us. He wore enormous brass earrings which
weighed down the lobe of his ear, making a hole over an inch broad,
and round his waist was a girdle of brass wire, to which, at back and
front, was attached a small piece of dirty T cloth, which was all he
wore by way of clothing. The girls wore similar earrings and girdles,
as well as rolls of brass wire round the arm, so as to resemble the
gauntlet of a long glove. They all seemed to think something

dreadful was going to happen immediately, so I spoke to the old
man in a reassuring tone of voice, but he failed to rise to Malay, or
even to the most barbarous Sooloo *patois*. So I had to send for one
of the Tunbumohas, and after a short time and a little tobacco, I
put the old boy quite at his ease, and detailing quite a little list of
grievances which I promised him should be inquired into. He was
the only male in the house, the rest being away at work."

This was the only house they saw all the day. At
night they hauled the canoe on the beach. The men
made a fire, cooked their fish, made their tea, and
after their meal stretched themselves out on the hard
stones of the beach, arched a kadjan mat over their
heads, by way of a tent, and went to sleep.

" These open-air bivouacs are very enjoyable (when it doesn't rain).
The ruddy light of the fire; the rapid river; the dark background of
trees; the sense of freedom; the lazy attitude of the men, who seem
to know they have earned a rest and a meal; and the general wildness
of the whole proceeding, have a charm which only those who have
experienced it can understand. As for myself, I slept in the open
canoe under a kadjan like the rest. I here take the opportunity of
mentioning the absence of mosquitoes, and other insect pests, which
under similar circumstances are usually such a trial to travellers in
the tropics. These appear to be rare in this part of Borneo."

IV.

On March the 2nd, the little expedition reached
the junction of the Quamote with the Kinabatangan
before noon. This is quite an unexplored river, owing
to its interior being in the hands of a fierce tribe, the

Tinggalums, who sometimes make a raid upon the
Kinabatangan.   In the pre-smallpox days, there
were villages all along the river at this point, but
what few were left by that fell disease were killed off
by the Tinggalums, and the whole district is now quite
uninhabited.   "A fort erected at the junction to hold
these people in check, and a conciliatory but firm disposition shown towards them, would soon set a thriving
trading-station on its legs here.   The amount of valuable produce, such as rattans, gutta, and camphor,
that must have accumulated in these richly-endowed
forests must be very great."   Owing to the English
having come to the country, there have been no raids
out of this river for the last three years.

The expedition held on, the river winding through
trackless and untouched forest, with the exception of a
few old clearings, fast being overgrown, which were
frequently seen on its edge.   Mr. Pryer estimated that
they had gone close on three hundred miles and had
only seen three villages, Malape, Seebongan, Terbilliong, and Blut, and the Tungara house—"a truly
pitiable state of affairs," as he truly remarks, "on
such a magnificent river."

At midday they rested and ate. The men chose
for their cooking fire a secluded spot under an over-
hanging tree which was in full blossom.   Though
they had not seen a score of butterflies on the trip,

here gaily-coloured moths flew about in bright showy
clusters, a dozen together, and among them were
several splendid ornithopia. Mr. Pryer rarely goes
out of his way to dwell upon the natural beauties
of the country, but on this occasion he is eloquent
in his description of the mid-day resting-place and
the run along the river for some time afterwards.

"The three ornithopia which I saw here all at once were larger than
many little sunbirds which were hopping and fluttering about from
flower to flower, peering into their recesses with their sharp little
bills for the minute beetles and other insects which take refuge
there. I know that these birds were of bright and brilliant plumage,
but they always kept so exactly overhead that I could only see their
black outlines from below, and they might have been as sober coloured
as nuns for all I could tell to the contrary. These were about the
only birds I noticed the whole journey. Perhaps half-a-dozen times,
large kingfishers, of a beautiful bright blue, skimmed the surface of
the river and then perched and looked at us with the utmost indifference. The croaking of hornbills was frequently heard, and once
or twice the stray 'swish swish' of their wings was audible as they
flew by perhaps nearly a quarter of a mile off. These, with the few
monkeys already alluded to, were the only features of animal life
that presented themselves. Everywhere along the bank, the tracks
of buffaloes, deer, and pigs were so abundant as to form perfect
roads, but they only come out of the depths of the forest at night.
The calls of birds, however, are always to be heard. In this part of
the world birds do not seem to sing, but most of them have some
call, generally strange and peculiar, but frequently quite melodious.
Amongst others those of doves and pigeons are often heard, especially where old clearings are common. The call of the Argus
pheasant is easily imitated, and if given, is sometimes answered from
the forest, and I believe on one occasion Banjer would have induced
one of these fine birds to come quite close to us, if we had had time
to stay."

On this afternoon of the eighth day of the excursion
the expedition arrived at the first of the real villages
of the interior. It was pleasantly situated among fruit
trees, potato and other vegetable patches, and with
the forest for a background. A recently-cleared
hill a short distance off showed paddy, a foot high,
growing all over it, and on all sides were to be seen
the universal plantain. Underneath the house, in
a sty, was a pig. The people are Tunbumwah
Sundyaks, but whether converted to Islam or not
Mr. Pryer could not learn. If they are, he says, they
have evidently made a reservation in favour of pork.
The house at which he visited he describes as " dark and
comfortless," and that may be taken as a description of
the remainder. He found no betel-nut trees there, no
cocoa-nuts, no goats, and the chickens were very small.

" The absence of cocoa-nuts particularly indicates a disregard as to
food, which, on examination, I found to be the case. The Malay
races of these parts, or of Sooloo, and many up the Philippines seem
to attach no importance to the taste of food. As long as they get
the merest *something* to fill their stomachs, they are satisfied, and as
each man finishes stuffing himself, which is what the process amounts
to, he gets up and moves off directly. The ' social meal ' is evidently
quite an unknown idea to them. A Banjermassin Malay I met farther
up complained bitterly to me on the subject of food, saying that with
his rice he then had salt, but nothing whatever else, and that until a
few days before he had not even had that. In the Philippine Islands
I was once in the same predicament myself for several weeks. One
consequence is that the people get swellings, sloughing sores, and
similar kinds of disease.

During the whole of the ninth day, March 3rd, the expedition passed many villages, houses, and clearings. The houses were pretty thick along the banks all the way. The people seemed contented and healthy. Only one man, however, appeared to possess "a proper plantation." It was composed of about two thousand sago palms, thirty or forty cocoa-nut and penang trees, besides durian, buah, nona, and other fruits. The owner took a great interest in his garden, and Mr. Pryer promised to send him some young mango and orange trees, a peculiar absence of which was noticeable throughout the Kinabatangan region.

"At one place we found two human heads suspended on a pole, in front of a house. I had heard that they were there before reaching the place, so going ashore, I entered the house, and its owner having been pointed out to me, abruptly asked him: Why should I not serve him in the same way? Hasah pricked up his ears, gave a fierce cock to his head-gear, brought his creese a couple of inches more to the front, and I heard him whispering something to Banjer about 'old times,' while the delinquent had an absolutely livid streak down each side of his face. However, at the intercession of some of the village fathers, I consented to reserve the matter for a bichara on a future day."

V.

The destination of the expedition was Imbok. This important village was reached on the tenth day, March 4th, and the Resident of Sandakan was received with great rejoicing. Questions of local

interest were laid before him in his magisterial
capacity, for the Company and its authority had been
well proclaimed and accepted. A curious application
among others was made from an inferior tribe, who
" wanted a slave to semungup." Mr. Pryer, it need
hardly be stated, rejected the demand, and treated the
natives to some explanations of the white man's views
of humanity and civilisation.

"I must say I rather liked the people at this place. The chiefs
and men were a lithe, active, leopardlike lot ; very light brown
colour ; wearing their hair about fifteen inches long, hanging down
over their shoulders, in the same way as I have seen the Sarawak
Dayaks do; but whereas in their case it has an uncouth effect, here it
seemed to add a grace to the people. They also had a cheerful
springy sort of way of setting about things, that was quite taking.
Their dresses were very brilliant. The Pangeran himself had on
green silk trousers and a yellow silk jacket. Among other costumes
I noticed a red jacket and yellow trousers; a blue jacket and red
trousers, and other similarly strikingly-coloured garments, the
material being chintz. I felt rather overpowered by all this magnificence, and was quite relieved when I saw Banjer come in, garbed in
a sky-blue jacket and scarlet trousers, a yellow sash with a very big
creese in it, and a head handkerchief of many colours with a tag of
it sticking up over his left ear in a most knowing style. I felt he
was doing his duty and 'keeping up on end' in a conscientious
manner."

The chief's house at Imbok is situated on a hill.
It commands a birdseye view of the river. The
scene is very picturesque, with its vista of banks
lined with plantations, houses, and fruit trees, and the

forest as a continual background. There are a few
hills, but the country may be described as flat. The
whole of the opposite horizon to the north is bounded
by a bold range of mountains some 2500 feet high
and about eighteen or twenty miles long. These
mountains, it struck Mr. Pryer, would be just what
would be required for tea, coffee, or cinchona, and he
picked out some plateaux at a high elevation as
capital sites for plantations. When he asked about
the hills, the people, strange to say, said there were
tigers there, and that they dare not go to them. By
tigers, Mr. Pryer believes they mean " the small and
comparatively harmless clouded tiger." Of other
animals there is a profusion in this district. Elephants
are rather commoner lower down the river, but
buffaloes, deer, pigs, and rhinoceroses are abundant.
In the fruit season, the Pangeran says, rhinoceroses
come quite commonly underneath the fruit trees, particularly the durian. There are also bears, but small
in size. A fair example of them may be seen in the
Zoological Gardens, Regent's Park. It is a bow-
legged, comical-looking animal, remarkably insignificant when compared with its neighbours from Asia
and America. Mr. Pryer saw many monkeys, but
only one orang-outang. Before he could get his rifle
ready, however, the creature was gone, although at
one time the Resident was within ten yards of him.

"What struck me most about him," he says, "was that he was almost black instead of the usual red. That evening I was told, in a house we came to, that a short time before a Soolooman, armed with gun and creese, walking in the forest, was suddenly seized by one, which tore off all his clothes and threw away his weapons, but did no further harm to him. He ran off as hard as he could, and fainted just as he reached his house. The animal to be really feared in these parts is the crocodile." The Resident thinks that good sport might be had among the deer. At one place where the expedition stopped on the return journey, there were three deer calling from the opposite side of the river not two hundred yards away. A boat floating down the river (with a "fire pan" in it) would be sure to run into favourable opportunities for its occupants to use their rifles. "Indeed," says Mr. Pryer, "for anyone fond of sport or natural history, I cannot imagine a pleasanter or more inexpensive trip than floating down the Kinabatangan on a 'lanteen,' and stopping at any spot required. Provisions, etc. could be sent up by canoe previously, and everything got ready with but little trouble."

How long a time will it take, one cannot help wondering, for the new territory to be sufficiently well known for shooting and fishing parties to be

L

familiar in this country of "unknown tongues" and people? Mr. Pryer himself offers some suggestive forecasts of the future of many of the deserted villages which he passed in the first days of his excursion. Smallpox and other diseases incidental to savage life, as well as hostile incursions in the olden days, had carried off such of the former inhabitants of these deserted homes as had not left for "fresh woods and pastures new." Mr. Pryer thinks an instructive lesson may be read in this episode of Bornean history. The natives who have thus disappeared were, "in some respects, civilised; could read, write, and argue; wore well-made clothes of cotton and silk. The general level of intelligence amongst the Sooloos is at least higher than that of the English rustic, and yet they have disappeared so utterly, that fifty years hence all traces of them will be entirely lost, and their clearings again covered with young forest trees. Suppose that in some few years' time, as seems likely to be the case, the irrepressible Chinese appear on the scene, clear the forest, and cultivate the ground: they will know nothing about this recently vanished race whose few remnants will mix in with the new comers, and the faintest traditions of the past will be obliterated."

If the judgment of Eastern travellers and ethnological experts is to be depended upon, the outlook so well sketched in these closing sentences is one that will be quickly realised under a vigorous adminis- trative, backed with the capital of a great and powerful company.

VI.

RIGHT ACROSS BORNEO.

From Marudu Bay to Sandakan—Incidents and Discoveries *en route*
—Sharks and Crocodiles—Enormous Gutta Trees—Native
Peculiarities—Tattooing and Head-hunting—Omens—"Bad
Birds"—Relics of Slavery—General Kindness and Hospitality
of the Natives—Adventures Afloat and Ashore—Song and
Dance—Capsized and in Danger—Native Patience under Diffi-
culties—Hungry and Forlorn—Rescued—"All's Well that
Ends Well."

I.

IF you look at any map of Borneo, however recent,
outside the one which accompanies the present work,
you will the better understand the geographical importance of the expedition across North Borneo which
Mr. F. Witti made from May 13th to June 17th, 1881.
The interest of the trip as a chapter of modern travel
and an episode of current progress, will similarly be
best appreciated by the student who has mastered
such history of the island as our literature possesses,
or by the traveller who has navigated the China and
Scoloo Seas.

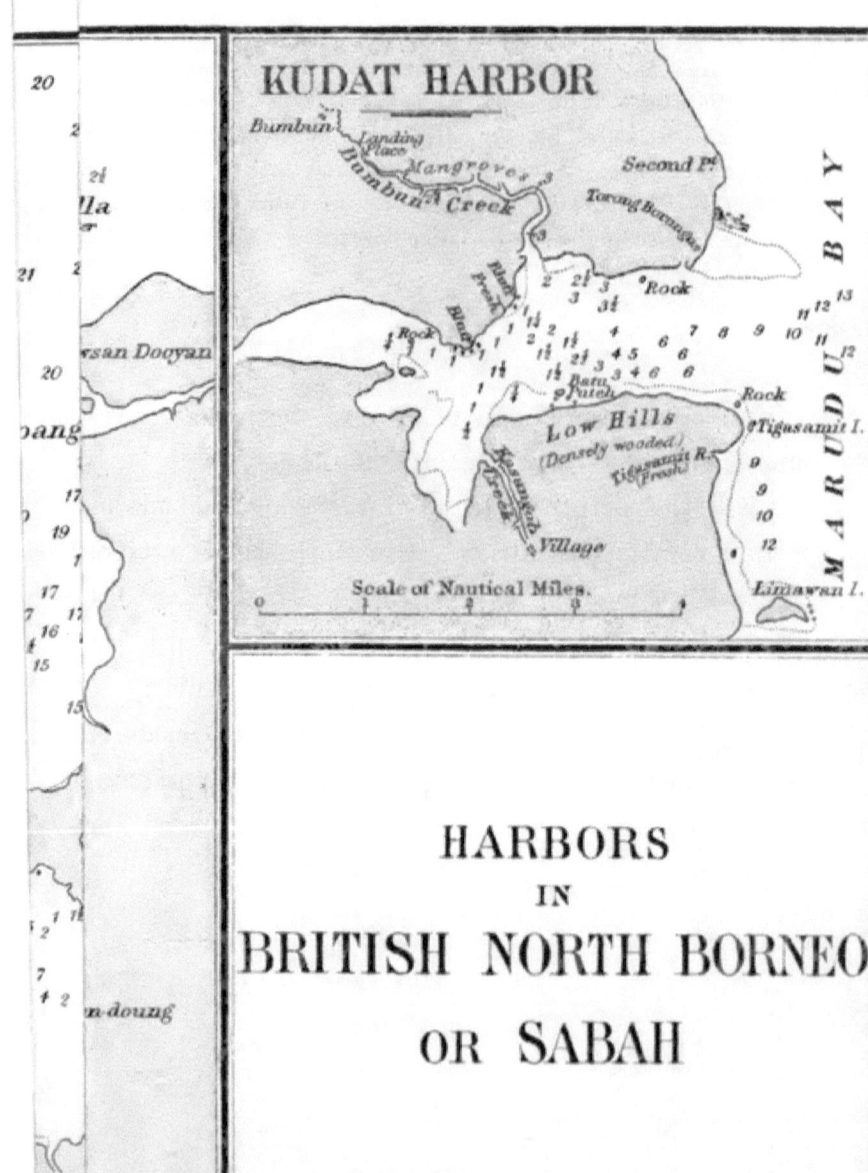

KUDAT HARBOR

Bumbun

Landing Place

Mangroves

Bumbun Creek

Second Pt

Torong Borongan

Rock

MARUDU BAY

san Dooyan

Rock

Black Creek

Rock

Batu Puteh

Low Hills
(Densely wooded)

Tigasamit R.
Fresh

Rock

Tigasamit I.

Marunga Creek

Village

Limawan I.

Scale of Nautical Miles.

HARBORS
IN
BRITISH NORTH BORNEO
OR SABAH

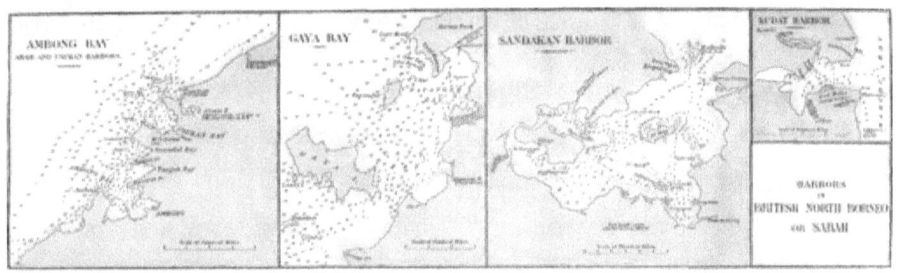

AMBONG BAY
ABAI AND USUKAN HARBORS

GAYA BAY

SANDAKAN HARBOR

KUDAT HARBOR

HARBORS
IN
BRITISH NORTH BORNEO
OR SABAH

London: Published for the British North Borneo Company by Edward Stanford, 12 Charing Cross.

Mr. Witti left Bongon, Marudu Bay, on the 13th of May. A journey of two hours and a half brought him to Kalimo, a village which is "ruled over by Sheriff Loya, a woman." She received him with a brief address of welcome and confidence. "I do not run away from you," she said, "as my brother, Sheriff Yassin, told me I need not do so." With this she pressed the traveller's hand and gave him the friendly offering of two eggs. He found that the crocodiles hereabouts have a reputation for that peculiar harmlessness which has been mentioned in previous chapters. "This reminds me," he says, "how one night we were fording a muddy creek near Ambong. The water there was beautifully phosphorescent; all of a sudden a crocodile rushed past that made me jump; but my guide, a Bajow, calmly said, 'Don't mind that; these crocodiles never bite you.' The Dusuns, near the west coast, are very fond of shark's flesh. On hearing a remark made about the diversities of a shark's living, they protestingly asserted that no fish ever eats man; only the crocodile does." Mr. Witti takes the precaution, which he recommends to other travellers, to steer clear of both of these creatures, and to be content, in strange waters, with a shower-bath on board your boat, and when navigating Bornean rivers to make your ablutions on the banks.

During the 15th of May, the region " pronounced

by a professional planter to be the Ceylon of the future" was passed, and the next day the village of Penenian was requisitioned for fresh water. "Penenian is a little community of Mamagun Dusuns. They live a quiet existence on the rice and vegetables they grow, on the fowls they rear, and never bother themselves about indiarubber and the outer world." Ascending from this place to the south-eastward, the traveller went through a heavy timber forest. On the road to Toyon the highest level above sea was 2300; Toyon is situated at 1800 feet. Kina Balu bears from here due S.W. In the vicinity of Toyon is Liput; and this is the Sonzogon country, the source of nearly all the gutta that finds its way over to Marudu.

"When emerging from the thick forest, what a burst of landscape! How the mountains crowd towards this peninsula! A coffee-planter would find it worth while to examine it. He could select his elevation up to 3500 feet, and the Bengkoka offers water carriage. The forest is partly the same growth as on the range between Tambunan and Papar. The soil is very porous."

The Marudu Sheriffs largely export gutta-percha. It is collected and dressed and sold by the Dusuns, and carried by serfs to the sea. The bondage system exists here, and under rather hard conditions for the slave. In this district the Dusuns call themselves Namagun, but by outsiders they are given the name Sundaya. They received the Company's representative with great friendliness. Their old man is blind. He said to Witti: "I have never seen a white man's face, and I cannot see yours, but I am glad to hear you talk our tongue."

A journey of three days through forest and jungle, and by several villages, saw the travellers in the country that is watered by the Souzoyon rivulet, an affluent to the Bengkoka, and is mostly jungle instead of timber forest. Both the gutta creeper and the gutta tree flourished abundantly. The latter, a Sapotacea, yields the stiff variety known in the Singapore market as Gutta kras, or Gutta merah (Gutta-percha). From the former, representing Roxburgh's "urceola elastica," is obtained the Gutta lichak, or Gutta susu, the Indiarubber proper. The natives extract the milk by a number of circular incisions from eight inches to one foot apart. The milk of the urceola was snow white, but of little consistency at the time. The stem in question was one foot in diameter, and but recently tapped. Among the Dusuns to the south of Kina Balu a fine is imposed for cutting a tree down; at the Upper Kimanis the offender has to pay a buffalo. "As gutta collecting gradually comes under the practical control of the Company's officers, a sort of jungle-conservancy might be established with advantage. Thus, the collectors ought to be taught the American (Parà) method.

Dusuns are a tribe open to sensible advice." In the jungle which was explored the next day Mr. Witti saw trunks of the gutta-percha tree having a girth upwards of six feet, and nearly a hundred feet in height. The natives here live chiefly on sweet potatoes and water. The returns for their rice and gutta they hoard up in the darkest recesses of the bush, consisting of brass in every conceivable shape— that is the only thing their heart is set on.

"Mount Kaidangan of the geographical maps is not known under such name either here or on the coast. There is a *rivulet*, Kaidangan, discharging itself to the north of Paitan. Over the position Kaidangan we travelled yesterday (May 19th) afternoon. There we were 2000 feet above the sea, but the point was not conspicuous among its surroundings. At present I am unable to guess which mountain-top may first have caught an eye in the offing, of importance enough to have been charted as Kaidangan. The mountain descried from Tankal (Bongon River), in N. 106° (?) E., and called by the Dusans there 'Palin,' corresponds, generally speaking, to the tract of Palin we find ourselves in now, when, three days ago, we were nearing Toyon we had a glimpse of blue water. The bearings of an island answered to Tcegabu (south from Mallawalle)."

The passage of Nipis Nulu had been described to Mr. Witti, by natives met *en route*, in a very discouraging light. He found it beset with some difficulties, but not of a serious character.

Nipis Nulu is the top of a cone, of which (through consecutive landslips) just enough is left to allow of a footpath between two precipices. One of these falls off perpendicularly to a depth of perhaps 500 feet. "Of the top the natives assert that, in a strong wind, it oscillates, reminding one of the celebrated rocking-stones of Cornwall." Mr. Witti found its height, by Boiling Point, to be 2446 feet above the sea. Pailin and Waigan are situated at 1230 and 840 feet respectively. The vegetation is timber forest, but not so open as that we passed through of late. Sugar-cane attains here an extraordinary thickness. It is grown for immediate consumption.

II.

In approaching the Sugut (which is mentioned in the Diary notes of May 22), the country was found to be well watered, the jungle irritatingly dense, and the road through it abominable. Of the rivulets crossed, and partly traversed, the Longom and the Kavilian belong to the Melinzao, which flows past the village Tinagas and is received by the Sugut on its left shore. The main stream is still some distance off, but the district of Tinagas extends on both sides of it. Tinagas is visited by the Sooloo traders. The inhabitants barter jungle produce of every description for salt, cloth, brassware, pottery, and miscellaneous articles. At Likabao a small Chinese settlement is said to exist. The Chinamen do business principally in the rubber line. Likabao can be easily reached by ascending the Sugut. "We, on our part, shall next look to the country between here and Mokodao, the eastward point of our route in November last. Our visit then was reported to these people; and the character we were given as paying for everything we got serves as an introduction now." It is one of the encouraging signs of all the explorations under the Company that, on their second visit, the officers are received with increased favour, and that in some cases distant tribes go to them with appeals for extensions of the white government; while the inhabitants of the immediate villages, on the way, lay before the Company's people grievances to be redressed and misunderstandings to be arranged.

"In the diary of November last, I stated that the tribes to the east of Kina Balu surpass those nearer the west coast in a physical respect. And here I notice the splendid heads of hair of the male population. Their hair is mostly three feet long, and is worn tied up in a knot behind when at work or on the tramp, but when at ease it is loosened. It is a curious sight to see a number of men combing each other's hair, and forming a chain in doing so. But their hair is by no means so thick as to support the theory of an improvement of the Dusun race by a mixture of Chinese blood. Men and women alike wear the neck spiral, and the former also a closely-fitting spiral around their biceps. As a tribe the Tinagus Dusuns are 'Mamagun.'"

Mr. Witti gives many minute details of geographical interest, which, however, it is not necessary to set forth in this summary of his trip.

Between Nolumpis and Kagasingan the country does

not rise to more than 1100 feet. It is mostly covered with old forest, and well watered. On the fields around Kagasingan the nicotiana strikes the eye most. Badly cured, it yields a good second-class tobacco. The people of Kagasingan received the expedition in a friendly way; and when guides to Kirokot were asked for, they came forward, on condition that they might be back in time for a wedding that was to come off that night; thus both parties were satisfied. They arrived at Lansat on the 26th of May. It is situated on the right bank of the Morali River, a considerable affluent to the Mokodao-Sugut. The rock hereabout is serpentine. Between Mokodao and Lansat the country is almost flat, and on an average 1000 feet above the sea. "In the course of an afternoon and evening we made close friends of our hosts. These people are peaceful, sober, and tattooed. Headhunting has become obsolete among them. The crania*

---

* "Traces of head-hunting in North Borneo are very rare, and they chiefly belong to a past time. The practice still exists in other parts of the island, but only in a small way. It is satisfactory to learn from Captain Mundy's notes, in the 'Journals of Rajah Brooke,' that, even in the year 1840, the Bornean head-hunters of the Sarawak country respected the persons of white men and Malays. The following interesting 'interview' of a Dayak chief of great intelligence who spoke Malay fluently, is from the work above mentioned:

"'Did he know anything of God?' (Allah talla.)—'No.'

"'Did his tribe believe that anyone lived in the clouds?'—'Yes; Tupa lived there.'

"'Who sent thunder, lightning, and rain?'—'Tupa.'

collected in former times seem but little honoured, for they are kept in baskets, mixed up with all sorts of rubbish. Curious, that in sifting the human heads I came on the skull of a sun-bear (*ursus malayanus*)."

" ' Do they ever pray to Tupa, or offer sacrifice ? '—' No.'

"'' When a man dies, what do they do with his body ? '—' They burn it.'

"' Where do the dead go to after they are buried ? '—' To Sabyan.'

"'' Where is Sabyan ? '—' Under the earth.'

" ' Where is his father gone ? '—' To Sabyan. All the Dayak men and women who are dead are under the ground in Sabyan.'

"'' How long will they stay at Sabyan ? '—' Don't know.'

"' ' When he dies, will he meet his father ? '—' Yes ; and his mother and all the people.'

"'' Are they happy in Sabyan ? '—' Yes ; very happy.'

"'' If a man was wicked, would he go to Sabyan ? '—' Yes ; but to another place, and he would not be happy.'

" On being questioned about taking heads, he said : ' They always take the heads of their enemies, never of their friends.'

"'' If they met strangers in the jungle, would they take their heads ? '—' Yes, if they were strange Dayaks, but not the heads of Malays or white men.'

" ' Could they marry without first having a head ? '—' They could ; but if they had a head it was considered honourable, and any young woman would then marry them.'

"' ' How many heads had they ? '—'A good many old ones, but only three new ones.'

" ' Whose heads were the new ones ? '—' Brang heads.'

"(I was aware that the Brangs had recently been defeated.) Of their laws I could make nothing. If a man stole, he had to return the goods and pay a fine.

"'In case of murder in their own tribe, what did they do?'—'Such things never happened!!'"

Nerawang was the next halting-place. There lives here an old man who has on the left side of his face a fleshy appendage which, on closer inspection, shows the rudimentary features of a reverted face, without eyes and mouth-opening. This extraordinary growth is of the size of a child's head, and is covered with skin of the usual colour. At Mangilan—on the next day, May 28th, with fresh guides—they found that the main level of this district is 1200 feet above the sea; the ground rises to 1600 in two ridges which we crossed, and there are a few out-of-the-way cones attaining perhaps to 1800. Everywhere are traces of the migratory habits of the Dusun tribe: they shift their planting-grounds as shepherds their pastures. The Morali River at this place is a torrent. It should, perhaps, be remarked here that villages in the interior are currently spoken of under the name of their head-man, if such headman be popular, or if the village consists of but one single house. This custom tends to create a certain confusion, and one cannot too precisely ask for the name of the place proper. It is better to apply to the old man himself. Younger members of Dusun communities are often ignorant of the proper name of their native haunt.

"From Inowantei we carried off the whole male population as guides; that is to say, three men were handsomely recompensed in advance for taking us to Tamalau. During a halt, one of their spears, stuck in the ground, happened to fall down and to inflict a slight cut on the head of one of our men. The Dusuns, at first mortally frightened, composed themselves on our assurance that we would not hurt them in return. The wounded man, a Sooloo, was disciplined enough not to run amuck on the spot."

During the few days about this period of the journey the native guides wanted to turn back on account of "bad birds." Dusuns are superstitious in a great many ways. The bird-omens here refer to their note, and not, as with the Dayaks and Romans, to the manner of their flight. Each village seems to have particular good and bad birds of its own.

"Early yesterday morning some member of the lark family warbled beautifully, when the guides suddenly stopped. 'What do you think of that bird?' they asked me, who happened that instant to look at the compass. 'Well, it is a good one, I am sure.' 'Do you feel quite easy in hearing it?' they continued asking. 'I do; and now go on.' They obeyed, and I fancied they were persuaded. But on nearing the next village on the road, the Dusuns declared they would rather give back their fee than walk any further, on account of that bird. 'All right, we'll get fresh men in that village.' In fact, however, the same men took us as far as we wanted. Why? Simply because their 'good bird' made itself audible in time. 'On hearing that, we are no longer afraid,' they confessed when a hornbill over-croaked a whole congress of winged singers."

Travelling a little farther on the Linogu River, Mr. Witti noticed that nearly all the men of Tamalau are tattooed, including even mere lads. They are marked on breast, shoulders, and arms, the same as the natives on the Upper Sugut. But while with the latter tattooing distinguishes the hero of an inter-tribal war, here at Tamalau it signifies something very different. When remarking about these signs of prowess, they at once said their custom was different from the people of Bundo, Morali, Kagasingan, Lansat, etc.; and then a story was told which betrays a horrible side of the Dusun character, although the narrators spoke with a glee as children might in talking about their sport. They laughed good-humouredly at their guests' cross questions about slowly extracting blood from their victims, or preserving the heads.

" This ' costumbre del paes' consists in the following : When they had been damaged in their plantations and other property by the ' Sulug' they kill every Soolooman they can get hold of. The Mahometan chiefs, in order to keep the river open, then used to reconcile them by giving the aggrieved community some slave—to dispose of; this is done by tying the slave up and spearing him through the thorax, which accomplished, the men in the village each take a cut at the quivering body. Whoever does that has a right to tattoo himself. They afterwards bury the dead without retaining the skull, ' for the Sooloo chiefs do not wish them to do that.' They assure us they are not the same tribe who are reported as catching the blood of such victims in small bamboos on purpose to sprinkle it over their fields; but they are certainly the same people of which the Danao men, pointing to the E.S.E., said, ' Don't go here ; *they* are very bad.' Evils like that must needs be faced before they can be cured. We are now prepared to meet, south of Kinabatangan, two-legged man-eaters."

The cannibal, however, did not turn up. On the contrary, the travellers experienced nothing but hospitable and respectful treatment. Less than half a century ago, they could not have journeyed through some of the pit villages of England either as safely or as comfortably as they can to-day in the wilds of Sabah.

The river shores to the south of Tamalau are in places flat and overrun with Lalang grass. There are crocodiles hereabout, by which the Dusuns lose dogs, pigs, and their worthy selves, which may show that the Linogu is between this and the lower grounds by no means blocked up by shallows. Its generally considerable depth is also indicated by the river's name, for "Linogu" means a "deep water;" in Bajau and Sooloo, "Lingkabo." All the villages here are situated high above the river level: Inowantei, for instance, 500 feet; Tamalau, 500; Mirawandei, 700. For their plantations the people select localities hidden from view from the river; and the ascent is as precipitous as the descent. Asked why they perched so high, they expressed much fear of the Dumpas men, a Mahometan community midway, perhaps, between this and the sea.

" From here (Mirawandei) we see Kinabalu; its highest top bears 317°, and in 220° is the Wodan Mountain. The Wodan—the name sounds somewhat like northern mythology—answers exactly to the

northernmost top of the 'Backbone Range,' which is on the maps
drawn as if pulling up short on the southern shores of the 'Lake.'
I estimate the Wodan at 8000 feet; the same is very likely a centre
of elevation."

III.

Having descended to the riverside, the expedition
built rafts. On these they floated down until they
reached Si Hino's, a Suluman's house. The distance
is only five miles, the river gentle. Whenever shoals
occur there are also channels deep enough for small
craft. Si Hino's place was on our arrival converted
into a sick-room. The head of the party came down
in a delirium of fever. Some of his men who had been
sick were, however, now getting better. In a short
time Mr. Witti recovered. One cannot fail to notice,
in his provisioning of his expeditions, an indifference
as to his own requirements and comforts which almost
amounts to recklessness. An iron constitution and an
ardent desire to be continually moving especially
characterise this pioneer of the Company; but, after all,
the commissariat is an important function in successful
exploration. It is not every European who can live as
the Dusuns do; and it is hardly wise to overtax a
fine natural physique in competition with such unso-
phisticated "feeders" as the Dusun men.

On the 1st of June, the Linogu was reached, lat.
5° 38' N., having more than half the distance from

M

Dauao flowed E.S.E. and then S. A little below here (Mangkalabu), Si Hino says, commences the turn towards E., as corresponding with the mouth of the Labuk marked on the Admiralty chart. Kina Balu, throwing off his cloak of clouds, was visible at sunset in N.W. ¾ N. There being no track to the Kinabatangan, they had to descend the Linogu farther. They did so for twenty-one miles, and put up at a single house, called Liposu, for the night (June 3rd). "On what seems to be the lower limit of Sogolitan we noticed a queer exhibition of the animosity towards Dumpas. There a rope, *i.e.* rattan, was stretched across the river, from which dangled all sorts of friendly mementoes, such as sharpened bamboos, wooden choppers, snares, etc." At Liposu, where they stayed at night, the family by whom they were entertained would only take glass beads in exchange for their rice.

The gutta and camphor hunters, when at Koun Koun, dig out canoes, which, when not in use, they conceal in the forest. "For us, the question resolved itself into either doing the same thing or hauling canoes across the watershed. We decided on the latter course for palpable reasons." Punguh and Buis are the last non-Mahometan villages down stream; the inhabitants are Tambonuas. Rowing down the river, several groups of Dumpas men were seen busy in manufacturing the gutta of commerce from the produce collected in the adjacent forests. To them both the varieties are known. Also at Punguh several people from Dumpas were met. They speak Sulu besides their own idiom. To the S.S.E. of Liposu rises the mountain group of Meliao, the highest top of which may be some 4000 feet. Both the Mentapok and the Meliao are by the western and northern Dusuns believed to be as high or higher than Kina Balu. The Mentapok we could see this afternoon again. Its highest peak bears from here N. by W. ½ W.; it is very likely not above 7000 feet.

IV.

The arrangements for the purchase of three canoes occupied all day on June 5th. An important business was also to think of the sick companions. It was decided to send ten men down the river, and to enable them to procure a conveyance to Sandakan. To that end they were provided with trade goods and medicines enough for ten days, and with a Malay letter addressed to all the hajis and chiefs of the river and country Labuk, requesting that the men should be assisted in every way; and in particular asked that some craft should take them on to Elopura, where Mr. Pryer would defray the expenses. "To-morrow morning our two parties will separate; under the circumstances it is the best I can do for our invalids. The impression I derived from Dumpas men and the people here tends to quiet me on the point of safety in this river, between here and the sea. Then our men take four rifles and one revolver with them, besides so many krises. The leading man, Hussein, is also plucky enough to ward off any attempt at enslavement. The latter point is the only one that gave me any occasion for reflection. After what is experienced on the west coast, in the vicinity of a Crown colony like Labuan, my apprehensions will be understood."

In the district of Pugula Delamasan the natives well remembered Mr. Pryer's visit last year, and at one of the villages applications were brought before Mr. Witti in regard to local affairs which he undertook to report to the Resident at Sandakan. The house of the headman of Punguh, Pangerapan, turned out to be a very clean and airy abode. In the evening a concert came off, when a Tambonua song was sung in which some of Witti's men took part. The tune was monotonous, but the performance had a homely touch in it, for it consisted in the persons slowly moving in a circle around the Damar light. In doing so they held each other crosswise by the hands, as if "for the days of auld lang syne."

On the 7th of June the canoes were duly launched. During the next day "a nasty snag prepared us a regular mishap." The leading canoe passed it, but the other two capsized. The tide was strong, the depth two fathoms, and the crocodiles—well, they did not think of them. As it was, everybody saved himself, and all tried to save their wrecked chattels. The actual loss consisted in one basket of beads and brassware, one Snider rifle, two krises, one spear, and a couple of saucepans. This was not the worst of their mishaps. After spending the night ashore, the next day they re-embarked below some rapids, when behind a sharp turn, the trunk of a tree was all but blocking up the river. The current, setting at this particular spot not less than six knots an hour, threw the leading canoe athwart that mighty obstacle, upset it, and keel-hauled canoe and all.

"The loss sustained is more serious than that of yesterday; nearly all the instruments and medicines went to the bottom, to say nothing of private property. The other two canoes were some distance behind, and remained invisible for a long while. Our misgivings that they should have come to grief on a previous snag proved true. The longest canoe, very leaky, turned up at last, reporting that they had both capsized, and that the smallest craft, a new one though, had gone to pieces; men and stores were all right, and the men would close up with us on foot—in any case they would walk on towards the village, let it be for two days. I at once despatched the longest canoe down stream to try and make the village, pressing on as hard as they could, and to return with assistance. They were

given the great part of trade goods, and all the papers; rice
we retained, the little yet available, leaving them enough for
one meal. We on our part would wait for our companions behind,
and then arrange further. Three men thus proceeded in one canoe,
while four of us waited in the second canoe for the remaining nine
men. . . . From the morning's start, the rapids, we only covered
six miles; the nine men were cast ashore at about half the distance.
We shall extend our present halt over night. Here we sit shouting
for our friends and cooking for them. They have but little boiled
rice in keeping."

Disaster, not fatal, but serious, scarcely left the
expedition from this point to the close.

"*June* 10*th.*—Another day of trial. Towards midnight we awoke
in our leaf hut—swamped. The water had since nightfall risen by
one-and-a-half fathom. We retired to a higher level, the water
followed us. In the morning we had to run the gauntlet in our tiny
craft; no bamboo or other buoyant wood available to make it more
steady. For eleven cable-lengths it went on; at the twelfth we
were caught by the branch of some tree, which would be, perhaps,
eighteen feet above a medium level of the river. The struggle for
the canoe was short; we had to let her go and the rice-basket
with it.

"Among my men is now but one Illanun; two other Illanuns were
among the batch of invalids ordered down the Labuk to Sandakan.
It is characteristic that, while the Bajaus assist each other and try
to save our goods, the Illanun lets go everything and makes straight
for the land. The individual in question and most of us swim like
sharks; and yet, could you have seen these plucky Bajaus how
piously they thanked God for the preservation of their lives, and I
must in justice add, for that of their master! The Koun Koun in
flood is a wild water.

"We happened to find ourselves on the left bank, our missing
friends were said to be on the right one. Towards sunset we

prepared our usual shelter of leaves and twigs. Then there was a
hailing, audible from the river: we responded. In fact, we were
continually hailing and shouting all day long. We recognised the
voices as belonging to the nine men; they were on rafts. Two of
the poor fellows did not object to join us by swimming a pool and
climbing up a steep mountainside. In reward we had to disappoint
them: 'Can you give us something to eat?' they gasped."

On the next day the head of the expedition went to
visit the second raft. There were four men on it.
Three others had preferred to drift on a log, but had
not been seen since early yesterday. The raft of the
two men that spent the night with us was smashed.
After urging the men afloat to make the village, they
parted company. About two miles farther on, another
hail from below, and the four other navigators re-
appeared. They had been wrecked, and now preferred
to walk. Choppers worked a winding path through
the jungle; but in wielding them the hands grew
weaker and weaker. "What a store this forest is of
everything that makes a tropical dominion valuable
from the very outset! But there is in this glorious
waste of trees absolutely nothing which the *homo
sapiens* could feed upon in an emergency. It must be
understood that we were drenched to our very gunpowder." The Bajaus, bred in the jungle, were at a
loss, in spite of their many resources against famine.

"Then I told them we should keep to the river, where we could
make rafts of rotten logs that float, the fresh wood being through-

out heavy as iron. The men could not stand the continual 'up-hill and down-hill' any longer. 'Yes, master,' they said, 'let us cling to the river; it is so much easier to die near the riverside, if we have to die at all.' The European, hungry though, but better fed than they are, could here laughingly answer: 'We certainly have to die, but not yet.' In fact, we shortly afterwards reached a spot which was a former planting-ground. Among the weeds and scrub the Bajaus revived, and so did the undersigned himself: we were as good as grazing. Then we had a halloo from our three faithful companions that had escaped the flood and reached the village in safety. They were now in search of us, in a fine canoe, accompanied by Orang Kaya Binua, of Parayon. We all embarked, and descended to Parayon. It was late at night when we arrived at the Orang Kaya's house, which is the one situated farthest up the river."

The three men reported adrift on a log were still, however, missing, and Witti organised a searching-party to go after them. But the next day he learnt that they had been picked up, and, with the exception of one man, little the worse for their privations and "four days' flirtation with crocodiles." Four of the party were, nevertheless, unserviceable. Accompanied by Sawad, who possessed a knowledge of the native languages, he put them into a safe canoe, with provisions, and sent them on from Sabongan.

"15th June.—The diary is being written up on board of the Sandakan steam-launch. That came to pass in the following manner:

"Continuing this morning up-stream, I could see we had arrived at that stage when, on a pioneering journey, the men must be allowed a few days', say a week's, recreation. We should not need that had we the freshet of the river with us instead of against. I decided on returning to Sabongan in order to give the men a rest. At four in the afternoon we were just hunting for a supper (hunting sweet potatoes), when a steam-launch appeared at the lower end of the reach. 'What launch is that?' 'I know,' said a Sabongan man, 'the Governor is sending rice to Quarmote, where he has built a house.' 'Indeed, then we shall be able to get soon to Quarmote after all.' My men: 'Yes, master, let us go to Siboku.' The launch was soon boarded. I found Datu Kabugatan in charge—the same Datu whom I believed to be expecting us at the mouth of the Siboku. The poor man was all done up with dysentery. He is an opium-eater, without being a De Quincey, I am sorry to say. Hardly could he explain the point of his instructions. There was, however, a letter from Mr. Pryer, written on the 11th inst., the day when our Linogu invalids had come to Elopura (after having experienced friendly treatment throughout the Labuk). Mr. Pryer ordered the launch to intercept us. He calculated very well that we should emerge at Kuala Lakan, and would think of striking in again at Quarmote. His very kind note runs in the main as follows: 'I hope the steam-launch will pick you up all right. Please don't think of going over to the Siboku this time. I cannot at present send to meet you at its mouth. When you come here we will talk over a trip for some other time there,' etc. I presume there are political considerations that bring our journey across the Company's territory to an unexpected end."

The five men who were sent down stream on June 14th returned in the launch to the expedition, which returned to Elopura, Sandakan, Monday, June 27th, 1881.

During this excursion the Company's officer halted at something like thirty villages and passed many more. Nowhere did he meet with rebuff or obstruction. On the contrary, he received kindness and assistance; and whenever "the lords of the Company" were mentioned by the natives, it was with respect, with liking, and with hope of advantage from the government of the white man.

VII.

THE PIONEERS AT WORK.

I.

Just as Java is full of quaint evidences of a past civilisation, Borneo has ample indications of a previous era of prosperity. In Java, records of the vanished power are found in strange mementoes of brick and stone; but in Borneo the Chinese have only left traces of their commercial supremacy in habits and manners that have survived them here and there in a mixture of the races of men. Five hundred years ago Java was populated by a cultured people, who built magnificent temples and other architectural edifices. "It is a wonderful example of the power of religious ideas in social life," says Wallace, "that in the very country where, five hundred years ago, these grand works were being yearly executed, the inhabitants now only build rude houses of bamboo and thatch, and look upon these relics of their forefathers with ignorant amazement, as the undoubted productions of giants or demons." While there are no traces of building in Sabah, and no opportunities of classic comparison with Java, it is in the power of the New Company to emulate the modern civilisation of Java ; and in doing so they will first seek to revive those old days of Bornean prosperity of which all ancient travellers speak, and proof of which is continually cropping up in the history of current exploration.

"Java ; or, How to Manage a Colony," by J. W. B. Money, is one of the most interesting disquisitions on the science of government which has possibly ever been written. Mr. Wallace recommends the work, and concurs in its facts and conclusions. He believes that the Dutch system, as developed at Java, is the very best that can be adopted when a European nation conquers or otherwise acquires possession of a country inhabited by an industrious but semi-barbarous people.

"The mode of government now adopted in Java is to retain the whole series of native rulers, from the village chief up to princes, who, under the name of Regents, are the heads of districts about the size of a small English county. With each Regent is placed a Dutch Resident, or Assistant Resident, who is considered to be his 'elder brother,' and whose 'orders' take the form of 'recommendations,' which are, however, implicitly obeyed. Along with each Assistant

Resident is a Controller, a kind of inspector of all the lower native rulers, who periodically visits every village in the district, examines the proceedings of the native courts, hears complaints against the head-men or other native chiefs, and superintends the Government plantations. This brings us to the 'culture system,' which is the source of all the wealth the Dutch derive from Java, and is the subject of much abuse in this country because it is the reverse of 'free trade.' To understand its uses and beneficial effects, it is necessary first to sketch the common results of free European trade with uncivilised peoples.

"Natives of tropical climates have few wants, and, when these are supplied, are disinclined to work for superfluities without some strong incitement. With such a people the introduction of any new or systematic cultivation is almost impossible, except by the despotic orders of chiefs whom they have been accustomed to obey, as children obey their parents. The free competition of European traders, however, introduces two powerful inducements to exertion. Spirits or opium is a temptation too strong for most savages to resist, and to obtain these he will sell whatever he has, and will work to get more. Another temptation he cannot resist is goods on credit. The trader offers him gay cloths, knives, gongs, guns, and gunpowder, to be paid for by some crop perhaps not yet planted, or some product yet in the forest. He has not sufficient forethought to take only a modest quantity, and not enough energy to work early and late in order to get out of debt; and the consequence is that he accumulates debt upon debt, and often remains for years, or for life, a debtor and almost a slave. This is a state of things which occurs very largely in every part of the world in which men of a superior race freely trade with men of a lower race. It extends trade, no doubt, for a time, but it demoralises the native, checks true civilisation, and does not lead to any permanent increase in the wealth of the country; so that the European government of such a country must be carried on at a loss.

"The system introduced by the Dutch was to induce the people, through their chiefs, to give a portion of their time to the cultivation of coffee, sugar, and other valuable products. A fixed rate of wages —low indeed, but about equal to that of all places where European com-

petition has not artificially raised it—was paid to the labourers engaged
in clearing the ground and forming the plantations under Government
superintendence. The produce is sold to the Government at a low
fixed price. Out of the net profits a percentage goes to the chiefs,
and the remainder is divided among the workmen. This surplus in
good years is something considerable. On the whole the people are
well fed and decently clothed; and have acquired habits of steady
industry and the art of scientific cultivation, which must be of service
to them in the future. It must be remembered that the Government
expended capital for years before any return was obtained; and if
they now derive a large revenue, it is in a way which is far less
burthensome, and far more beneficial to the people, than any tax
that could be levied."

According to Mr. Money, Java was in a miserable
condition up to 1832. Poverty and crime, dissatis-
faction among the natives, failing means, and a yearly
deficit in the national income were features of the
general situation. A new system was then inaugurated
which in a quarter of a century raised the revenue
from 24 millions of florins (£2,000,000 sterling) to
115 millions of florins (£9,500,000 sterling), and turned
the yearly deficit into a yearly net revenue of upwards
of 45 millions of florins—equal to £3,750,000, out of a
gross revenue of £9,500,000. The reproductive expenditure for public works and for developing the
resources of the country was raised from a mere trifle
to over 2 millions sterling annually. The imports
were increased from $1\frac{3}{4}$ to 5 millions sterling, the
exports from 2 to over $8\frac{1}{2}$ millions sterling. The
population grew from about 6 millions in poverty,

paying a revenue of about 2 millions sterling, or
6s. 8d. per head, to 11½ millions of "the richest
peasantry in the East," paying a revenue of 9½ millions,
or 16s. 6d. per head. In other words, in twenty-five
years the new system "quadrupled the revenue, paid off
the debt, changed the yearly deficit to a large yearly
surplus, trebled the trade, improved the administration,
diminished crime and litigation, gave peace, security,
and affluence to the people, combined the interests of
European and Native, and, more wonderful still,
nearly doubled an Oriental population, and gave
contentment with the rule of their foreign conquerors
to 10 millions of a conquered Mussulman race. The
only English aim it did not attain was, what the Dutch
had no wish to secure—the religious and intellectual
elevation of the native. But those benefits were all
obtained by means not only compatible with that
object, but which have involuntarily operated in that
direction, and have so far produced a firmer and more
natural basis for future improvement than is shown by
any of the results of our educational and missionary
efforts in India."

These benefits are due to the culture system,
"established by General Van den Bosch in 1832,
acting on the relics of the English rule in Java,
as modified by the Dutch on their return in
1816." Mr. Wallace, in "The Malay Archipelago,"

gives us some startling facts and figures up to a later date:

"It is universally admitted that when a country increases rapidly in population, the people cannot be very greatly oppressed or very badly governed. The present system of raising a revenue by the cultivation of coffee and sugar, sold to Government at a fixed price, began in 1832. Just before this, in 1826, the population by census was 5,500,000, while at the beginning of the century it was estimated at 3,500,000. In 1850, when the cultivation system had been in operation eighteen years, the population by census was over 9,500,000, or an increase of 73 per cent. in twenty-four years. At the last census in 1865, it amounted to 14,168,416, an increase of very nearly 50 per cent. in fifteen years—a rate which would double the population in about twenty-six years. As Java (with Madura) contains about 38,500 geographical square miles, this will give an average of 368 persons to the square mile, just double that of the populous and fertile Bengal Presidency, as given in Thornton's 'Gazetteer of India,' and fully one-third more than that of Great Britain and Ireland at the last census. If, as I believe, this vast population is on the whole contented and happy, the Dutch Government should consider well before abruptly changing a system which has led to such great results."

II.

I have ventured to reproduce these illustrations, as showing the possibilities that belong to a tropical country which has such splendid capabilities as North Borneo. It is quite evident that an undertaking of the magnitude of the new Company must have time to grow and give confidence to the capitalist, the planter, and the emigrant. Much less can be expected from the natives than has been got out of them, in the way of labour, by the Dutch. The Borneans are far more indolent in every respect than the Javanese. The policy of the new rulers of Sabah will therefore be to attract Chinese labour and Chinese settlers. Mr. Spenser St. John, when H.M.B. Consul-General for Borneo, came to the conclusion that Chinese labour would be the making of the country.*

* "The population of the territory of British North Borneo we can only guess at, but it is thought there may be 150,000 people, consisting on the seacoast of Malays, Illanuns, Bajaus, Sulus, and a few Chinese. In the interior there are a great many tribes who style themselves Muruts, Dusuns, Idaan, Booloodoopies, Mallapees, and others. These people seem to be a peaceable and agricultural race. The population can, however, be no more depended on for labour than the Malays in the Straits or the Cinghalese in Ceylon. In Ceylon all the estate labour is imported from India. We shall have to import labour in a similar way into Borneo, and for the purpose no doubt the Chinese will offer themselves in thousands as soon as wanted; their fitness for such work as agriculturists, gardeners, carpenters, blacksmiths, miners, domestic, and indeed, every kind of labour, cannot be gainsaid. Sir W. Medhurst describes them as being of a class sober, frugal, peaceful, reliable, hardworking, intelligent people, and in all respects superior to all other coloured races. It is those qualities that have gained for them pre-eminence amongst all other natives in Eastern Asia. In California and Australia they are much condemned; but it must not be overlooked that there they come in competition with white men as labourers. Moreover, they are subject to such certain bad treatment that only the worst classes will leave their homes for those countries. Let the Chinaman be known to his master personally, let that master treat him fairly, and there is no better servant in the world. At the same time they must be understood and checked

In his "Life in the Forests of the Far East," he says :

"There is but one people who can develop the islands of the Eastern Archipelago, and they are the Chinese. They are a most industrious and saving nation, and yet liberal in their households and free in their personal expenses. They are the only people to support a European Government, as they are the only Asiatics who will pay a good revenue. In Sarawak there are not above 3000 Chinese, and yet they pay in indirect taxes more than a quarter of a million of Malays and Dayaks pay altogether. There is room within the Sarawak territories for half a million of Chinese cultivators without in any way inconveniencing the other inhabitants; and these Chinese could pay, without feeling the pressure, £2 a-head in indirect taxes as those levied on opium, spirits, tobacco, and other articles.

"I believe, if England were to try the experiment of a Chinese colony where they had room to devote themselves to agriculture, to mining, and to commerce, the effects would be as great in proportion as those displayed in our Australian Colonies. The Indian Isles are not far distant from China, and emigrants from them are always ready to leave on the slightest temptation. I have lived so many years in the Archipelago that I hope my information may be found correct. I certainly expect much from the future of Borneo if the present experiment be aided or adopted, as it possesses the elements of wealth and prosperity, and can obtain, what is essential to success, a numerous and industrious population."

A traveller and experienced Eastern administrator who endorses these views (in a private letter, some points of which I have permission to use),

when in large numbers, and their own customs adopted as regards making their head men responsible for the maintenance of peace and order."—*Mr. Alfred Dent, at the Meeting on North Borneo, March,* 1879.

enforces his opinion with the following notes from
the latest Sarawak revenue returns :

" With a population of about 7000 Chinese the farms alone amount
to 88,000 dollars—nearly 90,000 dollars, or £14,000 sterling a-year.
In 1874 the farms amounted to 64,500 dollars a year, when steps
were taken to introduce Chinese to plant gambier and pepper. The
result has been that, with the immigration of about 2000 Coolies, the
farms increased, in 1880, 24,000 dollars, and the whole revenue to
230,000 dollars a-year (£50,000 sterling a-year), showing an increase
of 47,000 dollars, or more than £9000 sterling a-year."

Mr. St. John says every Chinaman is worth £2 a-year
to the Exchequer. In Sarawak, without any direct taxation, every adult pays the Government between £3 and
£4 a-year per head. With little or no capital, Sarawak
has therefore achieved great results, but it has taken
many years to accomplish them. Much more extensive and important results can be attained in the
North of Borneo, probably in a few years, provided
a somewhat similar system of government be adopted,
backed by capital.

To accomplish this, the first object of the Company
should be to organise a Chinese colony. North Borneo
possesses 20,000 square miles, more than two-thirds
of which is virgin forest, and a population of about
100,000, or five to a square mile. Java, on the other
hand, with an area of 37,000 square miles, about
double the size of British North Borneo, supports a

population of nearly 18,000,000, yielding a revenue of £10,000,000 sterling per annum.

In Singapore, where there are between 80,000 and 90,000 Chinamen, the yearly revenue, which is chiefly derived from opium and other farms, amounts to £200,000 a-year. Now there is ample room in North Borneo for 500,000 Chinamen, and it is evidently of importance that steps should be taken to induce their immigration.

In a paper read before the Society of Arts, Sir Arthur Phayre shows what satisfactory results have been achieved by a just administration of the government of British Burmah during the last twenty-five years. The population has been doubled, the revenue and trade quadrupled, an increased prosperity which is mainly due to the cultivation of rice. The climate and soil of Borneo are eminently fitted for paddy-growing, and there is no reason why rice and sago should not become the staple exports of the country. Whilst trying experiments with new cultures, the main object of the Government should be the employ-ment of capital in those cultures which are known to succeed in the island—*i.e.* gambier, pepper, rice, maize, and sago. A strong argument in favour of these articles, in addition to their adaptability to the soil, is, that the Chinese are experts in their cultiva-tion. The sago-palm grows to perfection in Borneo, and its culture gives an enormous profit. These are the leading suggestions in my friend's letter, and I print them for the interest that belongs to his statistics.

III.

I have before me the half-yearly report of the Resident at Sandakan, dated June, 1881. It is a record of the progress of the Company's new settlement of Elopura, and as a page out of the history of "beginnings" it possesses a special interest. Some day, when Elopura is a thriving city, these references to its earliest days will be read with curiosity and surprise. Just as at this moment Elopura is quite a wonderful little place to what it was a year ago, so twenty years hence its present size will be that of a dwarf to a giant. But as an example of how the new English Company is sowing the seed of a new world, the formal account of a Resident's stewardship at one of the newest stations in North Borneo is worth examination.

"The past six months," says the Resident, "have been marked by rapid progress in Elopura, progress more rapid than anyone could have been justified in predicting even in so short a time as eighteen months ago. This improvement denotes not so much an advance in Elopura itself, as an increasing prosperity throughout the country inland, Elopura being but the index of affairs generally in this part of Sabah." *

The population is permanently increased with the arrival of every steamer. Many of the immigrants go up-country gutta-hunting. The Chinese are coming in rapidly. The population generally is a miscellaneous one—Sooloos, Bugis, Sarawak men, Bajaus, Banjermassing and Manilla men, Tidong and Booloongan men. An attempt to take the census failed, but the inhabitants of Elopura now number certainly over 1200. Besides this, the settlers in other parts of Sandakan Bay are constantly increasing, over sixty-three arriving in one day.

" I may be pardoned for recalling to mind the time, not three years ago," adds the Resident, " when, there being an alarm of pirates at Balhalla, I went round the only three villages that existed then, and found that, besides my own one or two men, there were not even ten male adults in the whole Bay."

The health of the population continues to be ex-

* " The new town of Elopura is situated conveniently near the mouth of the harbour of Sandakan. It appears to be a very thriving settlement, being only thirteen months old. There are a good many Chinese settlers, and they evince confidence in the new Company's Resident by laying out a good deal of money."—" Observations on the North Coast of Borneo," by Commander C. Johnstone, of the Elgeria, September 4th, 1880.

tremely good. There is not a single case of fever of local origin since the first tree was cut in the clearing, and both diarrhœa and dysentery are of very unusual occurrence. Invalids continually arrive from the Kinabatangan and other rivers, but usually soon recover, owing to the combined influence of fresh sea breezes, dry airy situation, and good water.

Nearly all the children in this place have been vaccinated, and Mr. Wall, the local doctor, "has also been up the Bay and vaccinated the Bajaus, but not a single case of the latter took. At Tuong Leet most of the Andy Goroo Malagong's people have been successfully vaccinated, and the Seemomal Bajaus as well."

Industries are progressing: at Pulo Buy plank-sawing continues uninterruptedly. "There are now two or three small carpentering establishments besides the original Pah Lings of which they are offshoots; there are four or five vegetable-gardens, and a new one is just going to be commenced on a more pretentious scale; several people are rearing chickens solely for sale, pigs are being kept, bananas are occasionally to be bought, and in various other ways things are beginning to get more comfortable. The Bajaus having abandoned fishing, fishermen from Labuan have had to be introduced."

There is also a blacksmith, a bakery, a washerman, and

other small industries, down to a little brass-foundry,
where brass Sirih boxes and other things are cast by
Sooloo workmen. In the industries of the future the
drying and salting of fish promises to take a prominent
place. The demand for dried fish to be taken up the
country by the various gutta, rattan, and camphor-
collecting parties, is rapidly extending.

"Trade increases and expands monthly; there are
now twenty-five different trading establishments here.
The most noticeable feature of this half-year's trade
has been the arrival of over thirty sea-going vessels
(prahus) from Pulo, Gaya, Seebutu, and other islands,
and even from Sugh itself, and a considerable increase
in business in consequence."

During the period in question there has been no
single crime of any importance. Summons cases for
debt, disputes over matters of all kinds, quarrels
between husband and wife, have made up the bulk
of the usual Court business; while one or two bank-
ruptcy and liquidation cases have exercised the judicial
functions of the Resident.

"The close of this half-year leaves matters generally
in a very satisfactory condition. The Bajaus, who at
first were inclined to oppose us, are now our friends, and
ready to aid us with their creeses; and the Sooloos also.
The Darvel Bay people, who required a man-of-war to
visit them less than two years ago, are now anxious

to submit to us and ask for our flag. Dato Israel, who has been in doubt about us till quite lately, has shown his goodwill by giving his active assistance in one or two matters that required some little time and trouble. The chief man of Paitan is acting unappointed as a collector of customs ; and the powerful Sheriff of Maludu Bay, quite unsought by me, sends down for advice in many matters. The Chinese are quite contented, and I have not heard a murmur from them since certain trade rules were altered to suit their wishes."

Inland the country is "ripe for the Company to collect a fair tithe of the produce, and the people up both the Kinabatangan, Labok, and Sugut, are anxious, and even clamorous, to have the Elopura Administration extended to them." Says the Resident, reflecting with laudable pride on the work thus accomplished : "It must be confessed this is a great change from the past, especially when it is remembered that the people dealt with are found to be unruleable by other nations ; and that the best of them are known pirates, and have customs and rules regarding marriage, slavery, and other things which are quite at variance with our Western ideas, but to have combated which would have immediately placed us at variance with the bulk of the population ; in which case our way would not have been so easy with regard to the inland taxation, if practicable at all, while planting would not have been possible ; so that a little money which has been spent from time to time, in freeing slaves and the like, has not been thrown away. As it is, the various conflicting interests of Sulu and Dayak, Bajau and Booloodoopy, Chinaman and Malay, trader and artisan, fisherman and coolie, have all been consulted, with the result that European planters can start planting to-morrow with as much security as though in an English county instead of in a country which three years ago was impassable by small parties owing to fear of head-hunters or village feuds, on whose coast it required a small fleet to move together to keep off the pirates."

IV.

With the examples of Sarawak and Java at their very doors, with soil and climate equal to Ceylon, with the resources of a great corporation at their command, and with the foundation of their past four years' quiet useful work to build upon, the nineteenth-century successor of the East India Company should achieve great things. There is more than one Eastern Question, and that which is developing rapidly to-day with the raising of the flood-gates of Chinese emigration is

not the least important of the problems, Asiatic and
Oriental, which will have to be solved by future
statesmen. The "fragments of two continents,"
which are known as the Malay Archipelago, have
"an absolute extent of land" little less than that of
Western Europe from Hungary to Spain. The Archipelago itself is over 4000 miles in length from east to
west, and is about 1300 in breadth from north to
south. "It includes three islands larger than Great
Britain; and in one of them, Borneo, the whole of the
British Isles might be set down, and would be surrounded by a sea of forests. New Guinea, though
less compact in shape, is probably larger than Borneo.
Sumatra is about equal in extent to Great Britain;
Java, Luzon, and Celebes, are each about the size of
Ireland. Eighteen more islands are, on the average,
as large as Jamaica; more than a hundred are as large
as the Isle of Wight; while the isles and islets of
smaller size are innumerable." It is in these regions
that eventually the Chinese must find an outlet for
their labour. The progress of civilisation cannot
continue to pass by these "islands of the sun" in the
coming days; and when the historian a hundred years
hence takes up his pen to tell the history of the
exploration and cultivation of the Archipelago, the
society of English travellers and merchants who
supplemented native labour with a systematic endow-

ment of Chinese industry and ingenuity, will, it is
hoped, furnish a chapter of important and valuable
results.

It is certain that among modern commercial enterprises there is not one which suggests to the specula-
tive reasoner, as well as to the practical philosopher,
more interesting possibilities than this mercantile
annexation of Sabah. If the present volume gives
sufficient data for a proper understanding of the
newly-created power, and an intelligent sketch of
the country and its surroundings, the object of the
compiler will have been achieved. In due course
other pens will take up the story of the New Company
and the New Flag. In the meantime the reader who
desires to increase his literary acquaintance with the
natural wonders of the islands that dot the blue seas
of China, Java, and Sooloo, will find ample satisfaction in the works of Spenser St. John, Brooke,
Dalrymple, Marryat, Boyle, Earl, Medhurst, Bax,
Keppel, Crawford, Colomb, Wallace, Mundy, Belcher,
Tennent, Burbidge, and Bock.

APPENDIX.

From the "London Gazette," November 8th, 1881.

Foreign Office, November 7th, 1881.

The following Charter has been granted to the British North Borneo Company, upon a petition to Her Majesty in Council.

VICTORIA, by the Grace of God, of the United Kingdom of Great Britain and Ireland Queen, Defender of the Faith.

To all to whom these presents shall come greeting.

WHEREAS an humble petition has been presented to us in our Council by Alfred Dent, of 11, Old Bond Street, in the City of London, merchant; the British North Borneo Provisional Association, Limited; Sir Rutherford Alcock, of 14, Great Queen Street, in the City of Westminster, Knight Commander of our most Honourable Order of the Bath; Richard Biddulph Martyn, of 68, Lombard Street, in the City of London, banker, a member of the Commons House of Parliament; Richard Charles Mayne, Companion of our most Honourable Order of the Bath, a Rear-Admiral in our Navy; and William Henry Macleod Read, of 25, Durham Terrace, in the County of Middlesex, merchant.

And whereas the said petition states (among other things) to the effect that, on the 29th day of December, 1877, the Sultan of Brunei, in the Island of Borneo, made and issued to the petitioner, Alfred Dent and another, or one of them, three several grants of territories, lands, and islands therein mentioned, and a commission.

And whereas the said petition further states that by the first of the grants aforesaid the Sultan of Brunei granted to the grantees co-jointly, their heirs, associates, successors, or assigns, all the territory and land belonging to the Sultan on the west coast of Borneo, comprising Gaya Bay from Gaya Head to Loutut Point, including Sapangar Bay and Gaya Bay, and Sapangar Island and Gaya Island, and all the other islands within the limits of the harbour and within three marine leagues of the coast, likewise the province and territory of Pappar, adjoining the province of Benoni, and belonging to the Sultan as his private property; and in consideration of that grant the grantees promised to pay severally and co-jointly to the Sultan, his heirs, or successors, the sum of four thousand dollars per annum; and by that grant the said territories were from the date thereof declared vested in the grantees, their heirs, associates, successors, or assigns, for so long as they shall choose and desire to hold them; provided however that the Sultan should have the right to resume the control and government of the said territories if the above-mentioned annual compensation should not have been paid for three successive years.

And whereas the said petition further states that by the second of the grants aforesaid the Sultan of Brunei granted to the grantees co-jointly, their heirs, associates, successors, or assigns, all the territories belonging to the Sultan from the Sulaman River on the north-west coast of Borneo unto the River Paitan on the north-east coast of the island, containing twenty - one states, together with the island of Banguey and all the other islands within three marine leagues of the coast, for their own exclusive uses and purposes; and in consideration of that grant the grantees promised to pay severally and co-jointly to the Sultan, his heirs, or successors, the sum of six thousand dollars per annum; and by that grant the said territories were from the date thereof declared vested in the grantees, their heirs, associates, successors or assigns for so long as they should choose to hold them; provided however that the Sultan should have the right to resume the control and government of the said territories if the above-mentioned annual compensation should not have been paid for three successive years.

And whereas the said petition further states that by the third of the grants aforesaid the Sultan of Brunei granted to the grantees, their heirs, associates, successors, or assigns, all the following territories belonging to the kingdom of Brunei, and comprising the states of Paitan, Sugut, Bangaya, Labuk, San-dakan, Kinabatangan, Mumiang, and all the terri-

tories as far as the Sibuco River, with all the islands
within three leagues of the coast belonging thereto,
for their own exclusive and absolute uses and purposes; and in consideration of that grant the grantees
promised to pay co-jointly and severally as compensation the sum of two thousand dollars per annum;
and from that date the said territories were thereby
declared vested in the grantees, their heirs, associates,
successors, and assigns, for so long as they should
choose or desire to hold them; provided however that
the Sultan should have the right to resume the
control and government of the said territories if the
above-mentioned annual compensation should not have
been paid for three successive years.

And whereas the said petition further states that by
the commission aforesaid, after reciting to the effect
that the Sultan of Brunei had seen fit to grant to his
trusty and well-beloved friends the grantees certain
portions of the dominions owned by him, comprising
the entire northern portion of the island of Borneo,
from the Sulaman river on the west coast of Maluda
Bay and to the River Paitan, and thence the entire
eastern coast as far as the Sibuco river, comprising
the states of Paitan, Sugut, Bangayan, Labuk, Sandakan, Kinabatangan, and Mumiang, and other lands
as far as Sibuco river, furthermore the provinces
of Kimanis and Benoni, the province of Pappar, and
the territory of Gaya Bay and Sapangar Bay, with all
the land and islands belonging thereto, and likewise
the island of Banguey, for certain considerations
between them agreed, and that one of the grantees
therein in that behalf named was the chief and only

authorised representative of his Company in Borneo; it was declared that the Sultan had nominated and appointed, and thereby did nominate and appoint the same grantee supreme ruler of the above-named territories with the title of Maharajah of Sabah (North Borneo) and Rajah of Gaya and Sandakan, with power of life and death over the inhabitants, with all the absolute rights of property vested in the Sultan over the soil of the country, and the right to dispose of the same as well as the rights over the productions of the country, whether mineral, vegetable, or animal, with the rights of making laws, coining money, creating an army and navy, levying customs rates on home and foreign trade and shipping, and other dues and taxes on the inhabitants as to him might seem good or expedient, together with all other powers and rights usually exercised by and belonging to sovereign rulers, and which the Sultan thereby delegated to him of his own free will; and the Sultan called upon all foreign nations with whom he had formed friendly treaties and alliances, to acknowledge the said Maharajah as the Sultan himself in the said territories, and to respect his authority therein; and in case of the death or retirement from office of the said Maharajah, then his duly-appointed successor in the office of supreme ruler and Governor-in-Chief of the Company's territories in Borneo should likewise succeed to the office and title of Maharajah of Sabah and Rajah of Gaya and Sandakan, and all the powers above enumerated be vested in him.

And whereas the said petition further states that on the same day the Pangeran Tumongong (chief

minister) of Brunei made to the same two persons,
their heirs, associates, successors, or assigns, a grant of
the provinces of Kimanis and Benoni, on the north-
west coast of Borneo, with all the islands belonging
thereto within three marine leagues of the coast, of
the said territories belonging to him as his private
property, to hold for their own exclusive and absolute uses and purposes; and, in consideration of that
grant, the grantees promised to pay as compensation
to the Pangeran Tumongong, his heirs or successors,
the sum of three thousand dollars per annum; and
the said territories were thereby declared vested in
the grantees, their heirs, associates, successors, or
assigns, for so long as they should choose or desire to
hold them; and they further promised to protect the
Pangeran Tumongong with kindness.

And whereas the said petition further states that
on the 22nd day of January, 1878, the Sultan of
Sooloo and the dependencies thereof (in the said
petition and in this our charter referred to as the
Sultan of Sooloo), made and issued to the same two
persons, or one of them, a grant of his rights and
powers over territories, lands, states, and islands
therein mentioned, and a commission.

And whereas the said petition further states that
by the last-mentioned grant the Sultan of Sooloo, on
behalf of himself, his heirs, and successors, and with
the consent and advice of the Datoos in council
assembled, granted and ceded of his own free and
sovereign will to the grantees as representatives of a
British Company co-jointly, their heirs, associates,
successors, and assigns, for ever, and in perpetuity all

the rights and powers belonging to the Sultan, over all the territories and lands being tributary to him on the mainland of the island of Borneo, commencing from the Pandassan river on the north-west coast, and extending along the whole east coast as far as the Sibuco river in the south, and comprising amongst others the states of Paitan, Sugut, Bangaya, Labuk, Sandakan, Kinabatangan, Mumiang, and all the other territories and states to the southward thereof bordering on Darvel Bay, and as far as the Sibuco river, with all the islands within three marine leagues of the coast; and, in consideration of that grant, the grantees promised to pay as compensation to the Sultan, his heirs or successors, the sum of five thousand dollars per annum; and the said territories were thereby declared vested in the grantees co-jointly, their heirs, associates, successors, or assigns, for as long as they should choose or desire to hold them; provided, however, that the rights and privileges conferred by that grant should never be transferred to any other nation or company of foreign nationality without the sanction of our Government first being obtained; and, in case any dispute should arise between the Sultan, his heirs or successors, and the grantee therein in that behalf specified or his Company, the matter should be submitted to our Consul-General for Borneo; and that grantee on behalf of himself and his Company further promised to assist the Sultan, his heirs or successors, with his best counsel and advice whenever the Sultan might stand in need of the same.

And whereas the said petition further states that by

the last-mentioned commission, after reciting to the
effect that the Sultan of Sooloo had seen fit to grant
unto his trusty and well-beloved friends the grantees
certain portions of the dominions owned by the Sultan,
comprising all the lands on the north and east coast of
the island of Borneo, from the Pandassan river on the
north-west to the Sibuco river on the east coast,
including amongst others the states of Paitan,
Sugut, Bangaya, Labuk, Sandakan, Kinabatangan, and
Mumiang, and all the lands and territories in Darvel
Bay as far as the Sibuco river, together with all the
islands belonging thereto, for certain considerations
between them agreed, and that one of the grantees
therein in that behalf named was the chief and only
authorised representative of his Company in Borneo, it
was declared that the Sultan of Sooloo had nominated
and appointed and thereby did nominate and appoint
the same grantee supreme and independent ruler of
the above-named territories with the title of Datu
Bandahara and Rajah of Sandakan, with absolute
power of life and death over the inhabitants of the
country, with all the absolute rights of property over
the soil of the country vested in the Sultan, and the
right to dispose of the same as well as the rights over
the productions of the country, whether mineral,
vegetable, or animal, with the rights of making laws,
coining money, creating an army and navy, levying
custom dues on home and foreign trade and shipping,
and other dues and taxes on the inhabitants as to
him might seem good or expedient, together with
all other powers and rights usually exercised by
and belonging to sovereign rulers, and which the

Sultan thereby delegated to him of his own free and sovereign will; and the Sultan called upon all foreign nations with whom he had formed friendly treaties or alliances, and he commanded all the datoos, nobles, governors, chiefs, and people owing allegiance to him in the said territories, to receive and acknowledge the said Datu Bandahara as supreme ruler over the said states, and to obey his commands and respect his authority therein as the Sultan's own; and in case of the death or retirement from office of the said Datu Bandahara, then his duly-appointed successor in the office of supreme ruler and governor-in-chief of the Company's territories in Borneo should likewise, if appointed thereto by the Company, succeed to the title of Datu Bandahara and Rajah of Sandakan, and all the powers above enumerated be vested in him.

And whereas the said petition further states that all the interests and powers of the grantees under the several grants and commissions aforesaid came to be vested in the petitioner, Alfred Dent.

And whereas the said petition further states that the petitioner, Alfred Dent, and his associates from time to time of necessity expended large sums of money and made great exertions in and about procuring the grants and commissions aforesaid, and putting them into use and discharging the obligations arising thereunder.

And whereas the said petition further states that the petitioner, the British North Borneo Provisional Association, Limited, consists of persons who lately agreed to join together for the temporary purposes of acting as intermediaries between the petitioner Alfred Dent, on the one hand, and a company to be incorporated (if we should so think fit) by royal charter, on the other hand, and of carrying on until the grant of such a charter the management of the affairs arising under the grants and commissions aforesaid, and who, for convenience of common action and for limitation of liability, have incorporated themselves under the general statutes relating to companies, that provisional association having for its objects as declared by its memorandum of association (among others) the following (that is to say):

To purchase from Alfred Dent his interest and powers in, over, and affecting territories, lands, and property in Borneo, and islands lying near thereto, including Labuan.

To acquire by purchase or other lawful means other interests and powers in, over, or affecting the same territories, lands, and property and interests and powers in, over, or affecting other territories, lands, and property in the region aforesaid.

To obtain from the Crown a charter incorporating and regulating a company constituted with the like objects as aforesaid, or other objects relating to any territories, lands, and property as aforesaid.

To transfer to the company so incorporated any interests and powers as aforesaid for the time being vested in the Association.

And whereas the said petition further states that all the interests and powers of the petitioner, Alfred Dent, under the several grants and commissions aforesaid, have been transferred to and are now vested in the petitioner, the British North Borneo Provisional Association, Limited.

And whereas the said petition further states that Association will, in accordance with its provisional character indicated in its name, and in pursuance of the express provisions of its articles of association, be voluntarily wound up in manner provided by statute as soon as a sale or disposal of its territories, lands, and property to a company to be incorporated (if we should so think fit) by royal charter has been effected, and will, after payment and discharge of its debts and liabilities, and after distribution among its members of the proceeds of such sale or disposal and of any other its assets, be dissolved.

And whereas the said petition further states that the petitioners, Sir Rutherford Alcock, Richard Biddulph Martin, Richard Charles Mayne, and William Henry Macleod Read, are, with the petitioner, Alfred Dent, the directors of that Association.

And whereas the said petition represents that the success of the enterprise in which the petitioners are engaged as aforesaid would be greatly advanced if it should seem fit to us to incorporate by our royal charter a company to carry on that enterprise.

And whereas the said petition further represents that such a chartered company would render to our dominions services of much value, and would promote the commercial prosperity of many of our subjects.

And whereas the said petition further represents that the petitioners are in a position to raise the capital requisite for the proper and effective conduct of the enterprise aforesaid, and they thereby undertake to do so on obtaining the grant of such a charter.

And whereas by the said petition the petitioners therefore most humbly pray that we will be graciously pleased to grant our royal charter for incorporating a company to carry on the enterprise aforesaid by such name and with such powers and privileges and subject to such conditions as to us may seem meet.

Now therefore we, having taken the said petition into our royal consideration in our Council, and being satisfied that the intentions of the petitioners are praiseworthy and deserve encouragement, and that the enterprise in the petition described may be productive of much benefit to our dominions and to many of our subjects, by our prerogative royal and of our especial grace, certain knowledge, and mere motion have constituted, erected, and incorporated, and by this our charter for us and our heirs and royal successors, do constitute, erect, and incorporate into one body politic and corporate, by the name of The British North Borneo Company, the said Alfred Dent, Sir Rutherford Alcock, Richard Biddulph Martin, Richard Charles Mayne, and William Henry Macleod Read, and such other persons and such bodies as from time to time become and are members of that body, with perpetual succession, and a common seal, with power to alter or renew the same at discretion, and with the further authorities, powers, and privileges conferred and subject to the conditions imposed by this our charter; and we do hereby accordingly will, ordain, and declare as follows (that is to say):

Transfer to Company of Grants and Commissions.

1. The said British North Borneo Company (in this our charter referred to as the Company) is hereby authorised and empowered to acquire by purchase or other lawful means from the British North Borneo Provisional Association, Limited, the full benefit of the several grants and commissions aforesaid, or any of them, as the same is vested in that Association, and all interests and powers of that Association thereunder, and all interests and powers vested in that Association in, over, or affecting the territories, lands, and property comprised in those several grants, or in, over, or affecting any territories, lands, or property in Borneo, or in any island laying near thereto, including Labuan, and to hold, use, enjoy, and exercise the same for the purposes and on the terms of this our charter.

Fulfilment by Company of Promises of Grantees.

2. The Company, as representing the original grantees under the several grants aforesaid, shall be bound by and shall fulfil the promises of payment and other promises therein made, subject to any subsequent agreement affecting those promises.

British character of Company.

3. The Company shall always be and remain British in character and domicile, and shall have its principal office in England; and all the members of its court of directors or other governing body and its principal

representative in Borneo shall always be natural-born British subjects or persons who have been naturalised as British subjects by or under an Act of the Parliament of our United Kingdom.

Restriction on Transfer by Company.

4. The Company shall not have power to transfer, wholly or in part, the benefit of the grants and commissions aforesaid, or any of them, except with the consent of one of our principal Secretaries of State (in this our charter referred to as our Secretary of State).

Differences with Sultans.

5. In case at any time any difference arises between the Sultan of Brunei or the Sultan of Sooloo and the Company, that difference shall on the part of the Company be submitted to the decision of our Secretary of State, if he is willing to undertake the decision thereof.

Foreign Powers.

6. If at any time our Secretary of State thinks fit to dissent from or object to any of the dealings of the Company with any foreign power, and to make to the Company any suggestion founded on that dissent or objection, the Company shall act in accordance therewith.

Slavery.

7. The Company shall to the best of its power discourage, and, as far as may be practicable, abolish by degrees, any system of domestic servitude existing

among the tribes of the coast or interior of Borneo; and no foreigner, whether European, Chinese, or other, shall be allowed to own slaves of any kind in the Company's territories.

Religions of Inhabitants.

8. The Company as such, or its officers as such, shall not in any way interfere with the religion of any class or tribe of the people of Borneo, or of any of the inhabitants thereof.

Administration of Justice to Inhabitants.

9. In the administration of justice by the Company to the people of Borneo, or to any of the inhabitants thereof, careful regard shall always be had to the customs and laws of the class or tribe or nation to which the parties respectively belong, especially with respect to the holding, possession, transfer, and disposition of lands and goods, and testate or intestate succession thereto, and marriage, divorce, and legitimacy, and other rights of property and personal rights.

Treatment of Inhabitants, generally.

10. If at any time our Secretary of State thinks fit to dissent from or object to any part of the proceedings or system of the Company relative to the people of Borneo, or to any of the inhabitants thereof, in respect of slavery or religion, or the administration of justice, or other matter, and to make to the Company any suggestion founded on that dissent or objection, the Company shall act in accordance therewith.

Jurisdiction over British Subjects and in Mixed Cases.

11. In case at any time we think fit to make provision by order in our Council for the exercise and regulation of our extra-territorial jurisdiction and authority in Borneo, and to appoint any of the Company's officers to discharge judicial or other functions thereunder in our name, then and so long the Company shall provide all court-houses and establishments necessary or proper in that behalf, and bear all expenses of the exercise of the jurisdiction or authority which those officers are so appointed to exercise.

Facilities for British National Ships.

12. The Company shall freely afford all facilities requisite for our ships in the harbours of the Company.

Appointment of Company's Principal Representative.

13. The appointment by the Company of the Company's principal representative in Borneo shall always be subject to the approval of our Secretary of State.

Flag.

14. The Company may hoist and use on its buildings and elsewhere in Borneo and on its vessels such distinctive flag indicating the British character of the Company as our Secretary of State and the Lords Commissioners of the Admiralty from time to time approve.

General Powers of Company.

15. The Company is hereby further authorised and empowered:

(*i.*) To acquire and take by purchase, cession, or other lawful means, other interests or powers in, over, or affecting the territories, lands, or property, comprised in the several grants aforesaid; or any interests or powers whatever in, over, or affecting other territories, lands, or property in the region aforesaid; and to hold, use, enjoy, and exercise the same for the purposes and on the terms of this our charter.

(*ii.*) To improve, develop, clear, plant, and cultivate any territories and lands comprised in the several grants aforesaid, or otherwise acquired under this our charter.

(*iii.*) To make and maintain therein roads, harbours, railways, telegraphs, and other public and other works, and carry on therein mining and other industries.

(*iv.*) To settle any such territories and lands as aforesaid, and to aid and promote immigration into the same.

(*v.*) To grant any lands therein, for terms or in perpetuity, absolutely or by way of mortgage or otherwise.

(*vi.*) To make therein exclusive or other concessions of mining, forestal, or other rights.

(*vii.*) To farm out, for revenue purposes, the right to sell, in the Company's territories, spirits, tobacco, opium, salt, or other commodities.

(*viii.*) To make loans or contributions of money, or money's worth, for promoting any of the objects of the Company.

(*ix.*) To acquire and hold, or charter, or otherwise deal with steam-vessels and other vessels.

(*x.*) To acquire and hold any personal property.

(*xi.*) To deal in merchandise, the growth, produce, or manufacture of the Company's territories, or other merchandise.

(*xii.*) To carry on any lawful commerce, trade, or dealing whatever, in connection with any of the objects of the Company.

(*xiii.*) To establish and maintain agencies in our colonies and possessions and elsewhere.

(*xiv.*) To act as agent in the region aforesaid for any other company or body, or any person.

(*xv.*) To sue and be sued by the Company's name of incorporation, as well in our courts in our United Kingdom, or in our courts in our colonies or possessions, or in our courts in foreign countries, as elsewhere.

(*xvi.*) To take and hold, without licence in mortmain or other authority than this our charter, messuages and hereditaments in England and in any of our colonies or possessions and elsewhere, convenient for carrying on the management of the affairs of the Company, and to dispose from time to time of any such messuages and hereditaments when not required for that purpose.

(*xvii.*) To do all lawful things incidental or conducive to the exercise or enjoyment of the authorities and powers of the Company, in this our charter expressed or referred to, or any of them.

Questions of Title.

16. If at any time our Secretary of State thinks fit to object to the exercise by the Company of any authority or power within any part of the territories comprised in the several grants aforesaid, or otherwise acquired under this our charter, on the ground of there being an adverse claim to that part, the Company shall defer to that objection.

Prohibition of Monopoly.

17. Nothing in this our charter shall be deemed to authorise the Company to set up or grant any general monopoly of trade; and, subject only to customs duties, imposed for revenue purposes, and to restrictions or importation similar in character to those applicable in our United Kingdom, trade with the Company's territories shall be free.

Deed of Settlement.

18. Within one year after the date of this our charter there shall be executed by the members of the Company for the time being a deed of settlement providing for—

 (*i.*) The amount and division of the capital of the Company and the calls to be made in respect thereof.

(*ii.*) The registration of members of the Company.

(*iii.*) The preparation and the circulation among the members of annual accounts.

(*iv.*) The audit of those accounts by independent auditors.

(*v.*) The making of bye-laws.

(*vi.*) The making and using of official seals of the Company.

(*vii.*) The winding-up (in case of need) of the Company's affairs.

(*viii.*) Any other matters usual or proper to be provided for in respect of a chartered company.

19. The deed of settlement shall before the execution thereof be submitted to and approved by the Lords of our Council, and a certificate of their approval thereof, signed by the Clerk of our Council, shall be indorsed on this our charter and on the deed of settlement.

20. The provisions of the deed of settlement may be from time to time varied or added to by a supplementary deed made and executed in such manner and subject to such conditions as the deed of settlement prescribes.

And we do further will, ordain, and declare that this our charter shall be acknowledged by our governors, and our naval and military officers, and our consuls, and our other officers, in our colonies and possessions, and on the high seas, and elsewhere, and they shall severally give full force and effect to this our charter, and shall recognise and be in all lawful things aiding to the Company and its officers.

And we do further will, ordain, and declare that this our charter shall be taken, construed, and adjudged in the most favourable and beneficial sense for and to the best advantage of the Company as well in our courts in our United Kingdom, and in our courts in our colonies or possessions, and in our courts in foreign countries, as elsewhere, notwithstanding that there may appear to be in this our charter any non-recital, mis-recital, uncertainty, or imperfection.

And we do lastly will, ordain, and declare that in case at any time it is made to appear to us in our Council that the Company has failed to comply with any material condition by this our charter prescribed, it shall be lawful for us, our heirs and successors, and we do hereby expressly reserve and take to ourselves, our heirs and successors, the right and power, by writing under the great seal of our United Kingdom, to revoke this our charter, without prejudice to any power to repeal the same by law belonging to us or them, or to any of our courts, ministers, or officers, independently of this present declaration and reservation.

In witness whereof we have caused these our letters to be made patent.

> Witness ourselves at our Palace at Westminster, this 1st day of November, in the forty-fifth year of our reign.

By Her Majesty's Command.

(L.S.)   CARDEW.

CHARLES DICKENS AND EVANS, CRYSTAL PALACE PRESS.

P